The Art & Science of Coaching

COACHING LINEBACKERS

Jerry Sandusky
Cedric X. Bryant

ISBN: 1-58518-171-4

Book Layout: Andrea Garrett
Cover Design: Laura Griswold

Coaches Choice Books is a division of: Coaches Choice
                                           P.O. Box 1828
                                           Monterey, CA 93942
                                           Web Site: http://www.coacheschoiceweb.com

CONTENTS

FOREWORD

by Joe Paterno

My involvement with Penn State football has extended more than forty-two years, both as an assistant coach and as head coach. During that time, we have had many fine football teams and produced countless quality football players. A major factor in whatever success we've achieved is the staff of talented assistants with whom I've had the opportunity to work. None of these assistants has been more devoted to the precepts of excellence or has exhibited a greater personal commitment to developing young men than Jerry Sandusky.

Jerry Sandusky is a man of high standards and deep-seated beliefs in hard work, dedication, and honesty. He has strong feelings toward America, Penn State University, and the community in which he lives. He gives of himself to others both on and off the football field—a commitment perhaps best reflected by his work with disadvantaged children with his Second Mile program. And, he is an extraordinarily fine teacher.

His coaching efforts with the Penn State football team have played a substantial role in our team's being awarded the somewhat facetious designation as "Linebacker U." The list of linebackers he has worked with over the years reads like a "Who's Who" of great linebackers—Jack Ham, Greg Buttle, Lance Mehl, Scott Radacic, Shane Conlan, Andre Collins, etc.

If you want to know more about how to develop linebackers, you could not learn from a better source. *Coaching Linebackers* will provide you with a detailed overview of the techniques and fundamentals involved in quality linebacker play. Jerry Sandusky is an organized, respected, and highly knowledgeable coach. This book is destined to become a fixture in the professional library of football coaches across America. It is my privilege and honor to recommend it to you.

CHAPTER 1

What Makes a Good Linebacker Coach?

The primary purpose of this book is to present a step-by-step progression for coaching linebackers. It is intended to serve as a basic guide for football coaches. While every coach has his own unique approach to handling linebackers, the procedures outlined in this book have proven to be very successful for Penn State.

The Penn State defensive scheme involves four linebackers who play a very integral part of our defensive pattern. A successful linebacker needs to be a multi-talented athlete who is able to defend against both the run and the pass. Quality linebacker coaching starts with an athlete who has the ability to perform these functions. An astute coach can, however, do many things to develop good athletes into great linebackers.

At the minimum, a linebacker coach should be able to:

- Evaluate his athletes' potential and help them to realize that potential.
- Develop and implement a sound defensive scheme that effectively utilizes the skills of his players and offers sufficient flexibility.
- Ensure that his players fully understand the specific responsibilities of linebackers.
- Explain the techniques that are required for his players to meet with the specific responsibilities of linebackers.
- Design and implement appropriate training drills for improving his players' linebacking techniques.
- Provide mental preparation for the various situations which may arise during a game.
- Analyze his opponents' strengths and weaknesses and effectively communicate this information to his players.
- Make necessary adjustments and offer proper assistance to his linebackers as specific situations arise during a game.
- Evaluate the total performance of his players.
- Offer valid suggestions to his linebackers for skill improvement both during the season and the off-season.
- Do everything possible to help his players reach their God-given potential.

Given the aforementioned steps, not surprisingly the primary role of a linebacker coach is to be a good teacher. His major responsibility is to help young men to mature and develop as people and football players. Every teacher/coach, regardless of the subject matter, should (to some degree) adhere to the following guidelines to be effective:

- Understand and clearly establish his goals.
- Work with the head coach and other members of the coaching staff.
- Believe in and understand the concepts that are to be taught.
- Analyze what he desires to convey to his players and decide on the most appropriate teaching method.
- Demand commitment and excellence from both himself and his players.

Contrary to popular opinion, successful coaches are not clones from the same mold. Individual differences among coaches often exist with regard to teaching style, discipline, motivation, etc. Effective linebacker coaches however, almost always will have certain things in common. They will be intense competitors. They will be hard workers. They will be enthusiastic. They will have a positive attitude towards their responsibilities in the athletic arena. Each of these qualities are traits that they hope to instill in their players.

CHAPTER 2

What Makes a Good Linebacker?

A good linebacker typically possesses certain character traits and physical abilities. Some of these qualities can be measured objectively while others must be subjectively observed. A coach should try to evaluate the total athlete and then isolate the areas that need further development and improvement.

Initial decisions by a coach regarding who should play linebacker are most often based upon demonstrated physical potential. Most of the players chosen to be linebackers should be good all-around athletes. For example, many of the outstanding linebackers in Penn State history have also been good basketball players. All of the great Nittany Lion linebackers have been able to move extraordinarily well. Among the physical attributes that "good" linebackers almost always possess are the following:

- Quickness (i.e., able to move from one spot to another in a short period of time).
- Agility (i.e., able to quickly change directions and move well laterally).
- Good peripheral vision—necessary to be able to see blockers, ball carriers, and pass receivers at various angles.
- Physical toughness and an eagerness for physical contact.
- Power and explosiveness in order to shed blockers and make tackles.
- Good speed and the ability to accelerate and overtake ball carriers and receivers.
- Instincts (i.e., have a sense for the flow of action or "a nose for the football").
- Good hands in order to be able to catch the ball.

A good linebacker, however, possesses more than certain physical characteristics. Many intangible qualities also exist that separate good or great linebackers from average players. In the end, the suitability of an individual to play linebacker is determined by his ability to consistently perform well on the gridiron, not by his untapped potential or by any particular physical quality he may or may not possess. For example, Sam Mills—an All-Pro linebacker for the New Orleans Saints—is relatively short for a prototype linebacker, but his "heart" and his play on the field override his lack of physical size. All factors considered, however, the best linebackers are usually:

- Able to recognize plays quickly, make the proper reaction and adjust according to the situation.
- Possessed with a feeling for the ball and the ability to translate that feeling into proper judgment when approaching a ball carrier.
- Consistent and mentally tough enough to overcome adversity and perform well under all circumstances.
- Able to concentrate under pressure.
- Aware of secondary blockers or receivers.

- Endowed with a flair for the "big play" and have the knack of being at the right place at the right time.
- Alert and capable of directing their teammates.

Subtle differences exist between inside and outside linebackers. Inside linebackers are usually more powerful, while outside linebackers tend to be quicker, faster, and better pass defenders than inside linebackers.

Few physical characteristics exist that are unique for linebackers. Ideally, however, a linebacker is someone who has the quickness of a defensive back and the power and toughness of a defensive lineman. Of course, each coach must choose his linebackers from the personnel that is available to him. Chapters #3-15 in this text have been written to enable you (the coach) to get the most out of your players. The techniques, information and advice have worked well for the Penn State program. Properly applied, they will work well for you.

CHAPTER 3

A Basic Game Plan for Success

A multiple eight-man front (eight defensive players around the ball) involving four linebackers is a basic defensive scheme which we have successfully used over the years. This scheme employs four linebackers (two inside and two outside) who can be aligned in various positions depending on the defense called. Having the ability to position eight defenders around the ball provides more immediate support against the run. The flexibility of the defensive scheme allows the team to adjust its defenses to many different types of offenses. Some of the basic different alignments which are employed from this scheme include:

SPLIT 6 (BASIC DEFENSE)

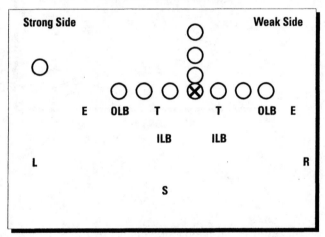

DIAGRAM 3-1

Advantages:
- The defense presents a look not often seen in college football.
- It is a balanced defense (i.e., equally strong to either side of the field or formation).
- The defense is strong against the outside running game because the defensive ends are aligned in a good position to immediately contain running plays in their direction.
- In addition, the defensive ends are in an advantageous position to contain the sprint-out pass game.
- It is relatively easy to game (stunt) with any of the linebackers from this defensive look.

Disadvantages:
- It is difficult to cover the strong side flat pass zone by an outside linebacker who is aligned on the tight end.
- The outside linebackers are not aligned in an advantageous position to support against plays that are run up the middle of the defense.
- Being a balanced defense, it is impossible to overshift in the directon of the opponent's strength.

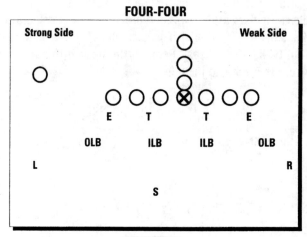

DIAGRAM 3-2

Advantages:
- It is a balanced defense, but the outside linebackers are in better position to cover the flat-pass zones.
- The outside linebackers are positioned in a more advantageous position to support against plays that are run up the middle of the defense.

Disadvantages:
- The alignment of the defensive ends and outside linebackers make it more difficult to quickly contain outside runs and sprint-out passes.
- Being a balanced defense, it is impossible to overshift to the opponent's strength.

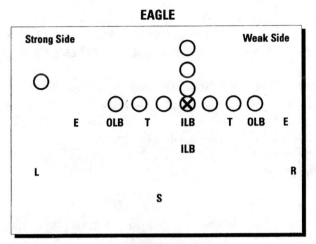

EAGLE

DIAGRAM 3-3

Advantages:
- This alignment has the same advantages as the split-6 defense. In addition, it usually causes opponents to adjust many of their inside blocking schemes.

Disadvantages:
- The same disadvantages appear in this alignment that appear in the split-6 defense.
- One less linebacker is aligned in a position to cover a passing zone, which makes it more difficult to play zone pass coverage.

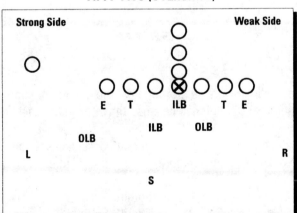

FIFTY-TWO (OVERSHIFT)

DIAGRAM 3-4

Advantages:

- The defense provides more support for the middle and off-tackle holes.
- This scheme decreases the number of seams in the defense because of the man on-man alignment.
- The defense is overshifted to the strength of the offense. This makes it an especially good defense to be played when the ball is on or close to a hash mark.
- An opportunity exists to have a balanced three-man pass rush.
- The outside linebacker on the strong side of the field is in better position to play the "flat" pass zone.

Disadvantages:

- Immediate run support is unavailable against outside plays which are run to the weak side (away from the offense's strength).
- The inside linebackers are not in an advantageous position to pursue outside plays quickly or get to their pass zones quickly.
- A defensive end must get involved in pass coverage in order to cover the underneath passing zones.

FIFTY (OVERSHIFT)

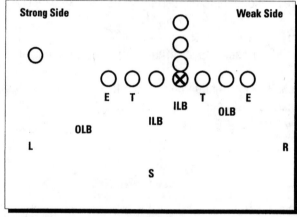

DIAGRAM 3-5

Advantages:

- This defense provides more support against the outside running plays to the weak side than the "52" defense because the outside linebacker aligns on the tackle.
- The linebackers are in better position for cutbacks because they are off the ball.
- This scheme decreases the number of seams in the defense because of the man on-man alignment.
- The defense is overshifted to the strength of the offense.
- The outside linebacker on the strong side of the field is in better position to play that "flat" pass zone.

Disadvantages:
- The middle of the defense is more vulnerable to the run because the middle linebacker aligns in a softer position (i.e., off the line of scrimmage).
- Immediate run support in unavailable against outside plays which are run to the weak side (away from the offense's strength).
- Except for the strong side outside linebacker, the linebackers are not aligned in a good position to retreat quickly to their passing zones.
- The inside linebacker who is aligned on the strong side is not in an advantageous position to pursue outside running plays.

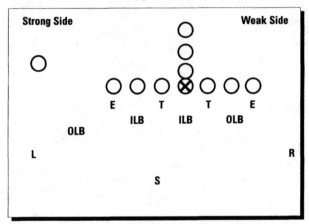

FORTY (OVERSHIFT)

DIAGRAM 3-6

Advantages:
- This alignment has all of the advantages of the "50" look while placing the inside linebacker who is on the strong side in better position to cover his pass zone and pursue outside running plays.

Disadvantages:
- The off-tackle holes are difficult to defend against the run because linebackers are aligned on offensive tackles.
- No quick run support is available against outside plays which are run to the weak side (away from the offense's strength).
- The middle linebacker and the outside linebacker on the weak side are not aligned in a good position to cover their pass zones.

Each of these different schemes will usually cause many blocking adjustments by the offense. They also provide you with the potential for a wide variety of games (stunts). If you use a multiple eight-man front, your defense can play with reckless abandon, however, your linebackers must be aggressive and want to make things happen. The flexibility afforded by this basic defensive scheme places a relatively greater burden upon your linebackers because they must be able to recognize plays from the various alignments. Having eight people around the ball also makes it more difficult for the linebackers to play zone pass defense because there are greater distances for them to run to their pass zones. All of those situations require that your linebackers in this defensive scheme must be alert, intelligent, and highly mobile in order to handle their assignments.

What Are the General Responsibilities of a Linebacker?

In order to understand the proper approach to coaching linebackers, it is necessary to understand the basic responsibilities of linebackers. Within a coaches' defensive game plan, each defense used is designed to stop certain offensive plays. Toward that end, the linebackers' assignments will vary with the defenses that are called. Some general assignments, however, exist which linebackers must be able to handle to effectively play within the Penn State defensive scheme.

Our linebackers must be able to:
- Diagnose running plays, provide strong support to the defensive linemen, and control their areas of responsibility.
- Recognize and quickly take the proper angle of pursuit against outside plays (sweeps, options, etc.). Inside linebackers pursue from inside to outside (refer to diagram 4-1), keeping the ball carrier on their outside shoulder (the shoulder on the side of the direction in which they are going). Outside linebackers should pursue straight down the line of scrimmage or give ground slightly once the ball has gotten outside of them (refer to diagram 4-2).

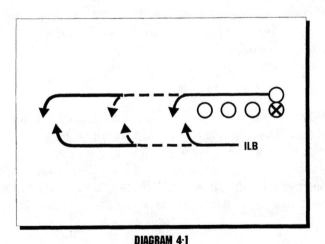

DIAGRAM 4-1

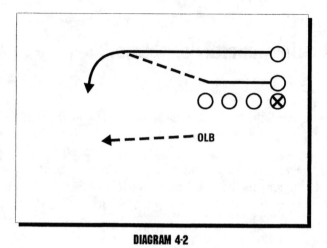

DIAGRAM 4-2

- Blitz (immediately attack an offensive area on the snap of the ball).
- Play zone pass defense (covering a specific area of the field—flats, curls, middle).
- Play man-for-man pass defense (covering an offensive receiver). In this area of responsibility, a linebacker can either approach his duties cautiously (covering an offensive receiver when you do not have deep help) or aggressively (taking away the passes in the area from the line of scrimmage to eighteen yards deep, knowing that deep help is available).
- Recognize the offensive formation and make adjustments to unanticipated situations.

The ability of each linebacker usually determines the defensive alignment. If all backers are of equal ability, it is generally most advantageous to simply align them according to sides (left and right). However, if your linebackers are more or less capable in certain areas, it may be necessary to align them in various positions according to the placement of the football (i.e., short side vs. wide side) or the type of offensive formations being used (i.e., weak side vs. strong side (refer to diagrams 4.3a and 4.3b).

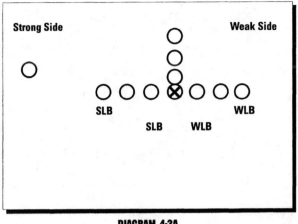

DIAGRAM 4-3A

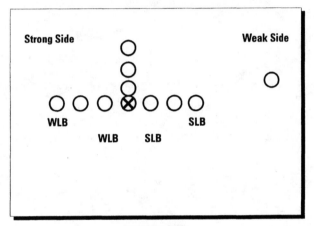

DIAGRAM 4-3B

Most commonly, two of the linebackers align to the strong side, while the others align to the weak side. The strong side is determined by the side of the field in which the offense has the most room to maneuver or the strength of the formation (refer to diagrams 4-3a and 4.3b). In the defensive schemes discussed in the remaining Chapters, the strong side outside linebacker will be referred to as the Hero (H), the strong side inside linebacker as the Backer (B), the weak side inside linebacker as the Mike (M), and the weak side outside linebacker as the Fritz (F).

CHAPTER 5

How to Play the "Split 6" to Perfection

The basic alignment in the Penn State multiple defensive scheme is the Split 6.   The numerous variations of the Split 6 Defense and the role that linebackers play in these defenses are outlined as follows:

I.   **Split 6 Rotate Defense***
   A. **Inside linebackers**
      1. Alignment rules:
      - Align three yards deep.
      - The inside linebacker, on the side of the flanker, aligns his outside foot on the inside foot of the defensive tackle (refer to diagram 5.1).
      - The inside linebacker, away from flanker, aligns himself by straddling the inside leg of the defensive tackle (refer to diagram 5.1).

      2. Keys:
      In order to diagnose certain plays, linebackers must be able to key specific offensive players. Inside linebackers read the near triangle. They focus on the ball but see the near guard and near back out of their peripheral vision (refer to diagram 5.2).

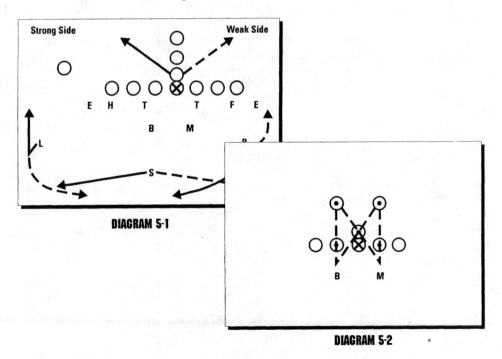

DIAGRAM 5-1

DIAGRAM 5-2

*Note: It is absolutely essential that clear instructions are provided to your players regarding the proper techniques for employing with the Split 6 Rotate Defense since it is perhaps the most difficult defense to teach and serves as a cornerstone for teaching other defenses from this alignment.

The movement of an inside linebacker is dictated by the movement of the near triangle. On plays toward the linebacker, he should slide laterally to get square with the offensive tackle and pursue from inside to outside. The inside linebacker's actions are dictated by:

- The ball coming his way (refer to diagram 5-3).

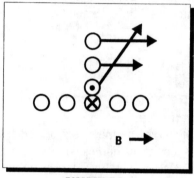

DIAGRAM 5-3

- The guard pulling (anytime the guard pulls he takes precedence over the action of the ball or the running backs) (refer to diagram 5-4).

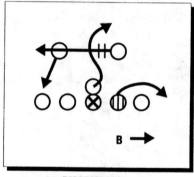

DIAGRAM 5-4

- The flow comes his way—the quarterback reverse pivots but both backs come in the direction of the linebacker (refer to diagram 5-5).

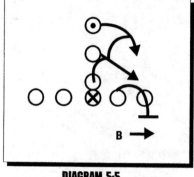

DIAGRAM 5-5

On action away from an inside linebacker, he attacks the nose of the offensive center (refer to diagrams 5-6a, 5-6b, 5-6c). His focal point is the nose of the center where he is aligned before the snap of the ball. If the center charges off the line of scrimmage at an angle to handle the gap on the side that the play is going, the linebacker should move behind the center and take a flat angle of pursuit. If the offensive center blocks the linebacker, the linebacker should square up against the center and keep everything on his play side shoulder in order to guard against cutbacks (refer to diagram 5-6d).

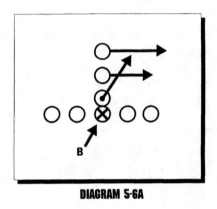

DIAGRAM 5-6A

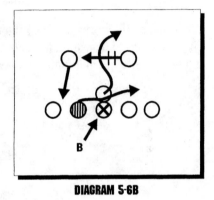

DIAGRAM 5-6B

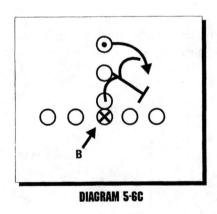

DIAGRAM 5-6C

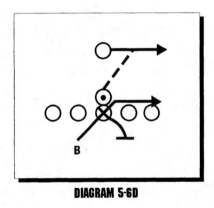

DIAGRAM 5-6D

Anytime the guard blocks out on the defensive tackle to a linebacker's side and the center attacks the other linebacker, the isolated linebacker should step up and attack the lead back (refer to diagram 5-7).

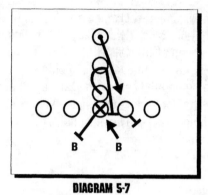

DIAGRAM 5-7

When the guard blocks down on the next man to the inside, the linebacker should either step up to beat the offensive tackle coming down on him to the hole or react to the opposite guard in order to play the block of the tackle (refer to diagram 5-8).

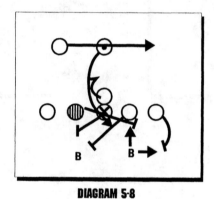

DIAGRAM 5-8

If counter action occurs in the backfield, the linebacker should not react until he can see where the ball is going. The position of the offensive lineman's head will indicate the proper direction (refer to diagram 5-9).

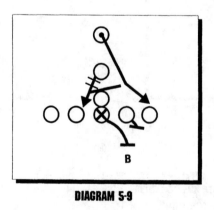

DIAGRAM 5-9

When the quarterback goes straight back or an offensive lineman sets up for pass protection, the linebacker should start to his pass zone but remain alert for draw plays (refer to diagram 5-10).

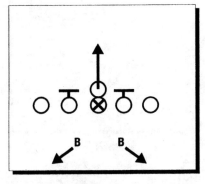

DIAGRAM 5-10

3. **Pass coverage responsibilities:**
   - Roll-out action toward the linebacker—slide, near hook or curl (refer to diagram 5-11).

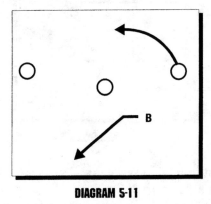

DIAGRAM 5-11

   - Straight drop back—curl (refer to diagram 5-12).

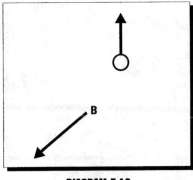

DIAGRAM 5-12

• Roll-out action away from the linebacker (refer to diagram 5-13).

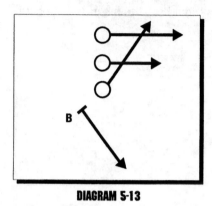

DIAGRAM 5-13

4. **Option responsibilities:**
    The inside linebackers are responsible for the veer (refer to diagram 5-14).

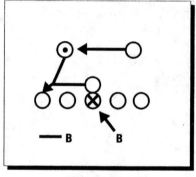

DIAGRAM 5-14

5. **Play is against two wide receivers—separated by more than five yards—to one side (twins):**
    The inside linebackers have the same responsibilities toward them (except on an action pass)—they must contain (refer to diagram 5-15).

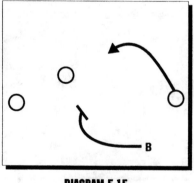

DIAGRAM 5-15

B. Outside linebackers

1. Alignment rules:

- Align nose on the inside eye of a normally positioned (one yard split) tight end .
- If the tight end splits out to two yards, align on the inside half of the tight end (refer to diagram 5-16).

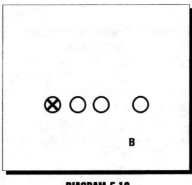

DIAGRAM 5-16

- When away from the strength of the formation and the tight end splits from two to three yards, the defensive end to the inside and the linebacker should line up on the tight end at a depth of two yards (refer to diagram 5-17).

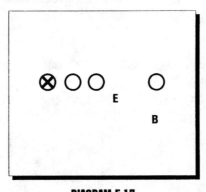

DIAGRAM 5-17

- When away from the strength of the formation and the tight end splits over three yards, the linebacker should straddle the inside leg of the defensive end (refer to diagram 5-18).

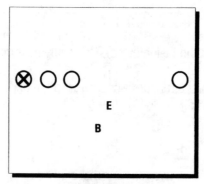

DIAGRAM 5-18

- When aligned on the same side as two eligible receivers (the strength of the formation) and the tight end or slot splits more than two yards, the defensive end should switch to the inside and the linebacker should move out on the inside receiver up to six yards from the offensive tackle at a depth of about three yards (refer to diagram 5-19).

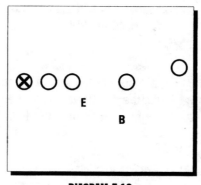

DIAGRAM 5-19

2. **Keys:**
   - The outside linebacker should read the tight end for his initial reaction. He should mirror the tight end for one slide (shuffle) in either direction (refer to diagram 5-20).

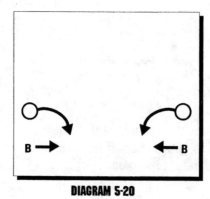

DIAGRAM 5-20

- If the tight end blocks the linebacker, the proper reaction is to get square with the blocker and be ready to move in either direction— most often, it will be to the outside (refer to diagram 5-21).

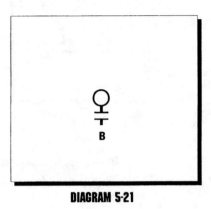

DIAGRAM 5-21

- After his initial reaction, the linebacker should then react to the next potential blocker or to the ball. If the tight end blocks out, the linebacker should slide with him, quickly recover to his initial position, and be ready to react to a kick-out by a guard, tackle, or near running back. He should keep his shoulders square, react to the pressure of the blocker, and give ground if necessary to come off a block (refer to diagram 5-22).

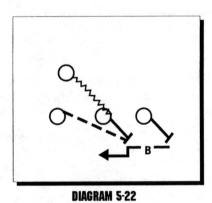

DIAGRAM 5-22

- The linebacker should never let a tight end release from the line of scrimmage to his inside without obstructing him. If the tight end blocks down, the linebacker should slide with him, recover to his initial position, and be ready to react to a kick out block by a guard, tackle, or near running back. He should keep his shoulders square, react to the pressure of the blocker, and give ground if necessary to come off a block (refer to diagram 5-23).

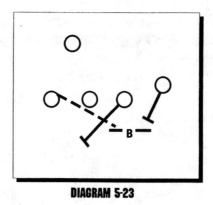

DIAGRAM 5-23

• When the tight end releases for a pass, the linebacker should slide with him and then react to the action of the quarterback (refer to diagram 5-24).

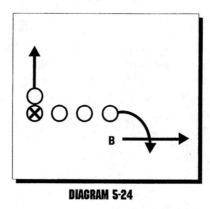

DIAGRAM 5-24

• When aligned on the side of the formation that does not have a tight end, the linebacker should key through the offensive tackle to the ball (refer to diagram 5-25).

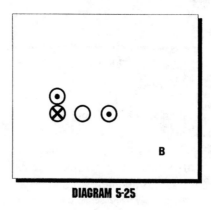

DIAGRAM 5-25

3. Pass coverage responsibilities:

- Roll-out action toward the linebacker—rush with reckless abandon to the quarterback (refer to diagram 5-26).

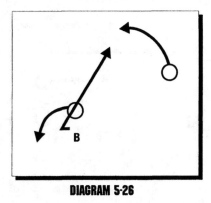

DIAGRAM 5-26

- Straight drop back—cover the flat (refer to diagram 5-27).

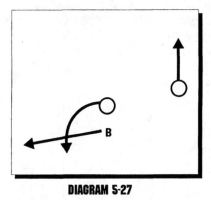

DIAGRAM 5-27

- Action away from the linebacker—cover the deep seam, pivot to the inside and come straight back (refer to diagram 5-28).

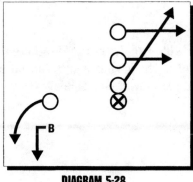

DIAGRAM 5-28

4. Option responsibilities:

- Against the down the line option (no junction between the quarterback and a running back), the outside linebackers are responsible for the quarterback (refer to diagram 5-29).

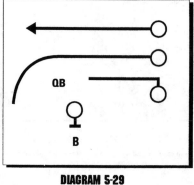

DIAGRAM 5-29

- Against hook-up option, the outside linebackers are responsible for whoever comes through the area from the outside half of the offensive tackle to the inside half of the tight end with the ball—veer or quarterback (refer to diagrams 5-30a and 5-30b).

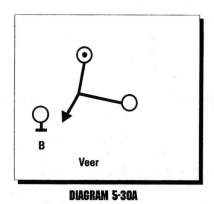

| DIAGRAM 5-30A | DIAGRAM 5-30B |

5. Play versus two wide receivers (separated by more than five yards) to one side (twins): The outside linebackers cover the curl pass zone versus a sprint out pass toward the side of the two wide receivers (refer to diagram 5-31).

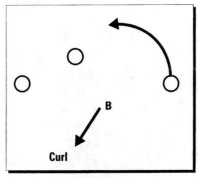

DIAGRAM 5-31

II. Split 6 (Roll to two deep zone defense coverage versus a drop back pass)

The responsibilities are the same for the linebackers as in rotate coverage, except on a drop back pass the outside linebacker on the strong side of formation plays curl, the inside linebacker on the strong side of formation plays middle, the inside linebacker away from the strong side of formation plays the curl, and the outside linebacker away from the strong side of formation plays the flat. This coverage makes it possible to cover all five of the underneath pass zones versus a drop back pass (refer to diagram 5-32).

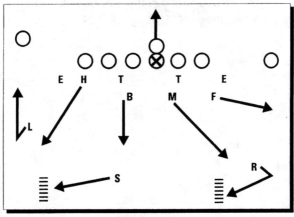

DIAGRAM 5-32

III. Split 6 Reckless Man Defense (Two deep reckless man-for-man coverage)

The responsibilities for the linebackers are the same as the two deep zone coverage, except against all passes the outside linebacker on the strong side of the formation plays #2 reckless man-for-man, the inside linebacker on the strong side of the formation plays #3 reckless man-for-man, the inside linebacker away from the strong side of the formation plays #4 reckless man-for-man, and the outside linebacker away from the strong side of the formation plays #5 reckless man-for-man. This coverage provides a change up to handle all of the receivers man-for-man yet still provide help against deep passes (refer to diagram 5-33).

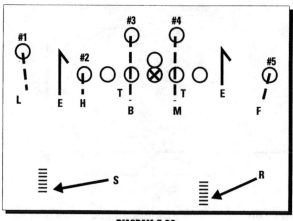

DIAGRAM 5-33

IV. Split 6 Blitz Defense

The inside linebackers charge straight forward on the snap of the ball. Although they try to penetrate across the line of scrimmage, they must read the play on the run. As soon as they diagnose the play or get blocked, they should adjust their course. The weak side outside linebacker should play #4 cautious man-for-man against a pass, while the outside linebacker on the strong side of the formation will either play #2 cautious man-for-man or curl versus a pass depending on the coverage (refer to diagram 5-34).

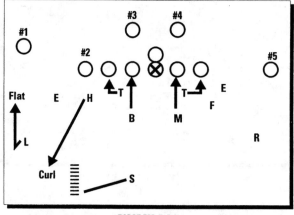

DIAGRAM 5-34

V. Split 6 Blow Defense

The outside linebackers charge directly behind the buttocks of the offensive tackles. Against a normal tight end (one yard split), they should open step to the inside and then come straight up the field. If the split of the tight end is over one yard, they should charge directly to their penetration point. If the split is less than one yard, they should switch assignments with the defensive end and step outside the end, move up field, and contain the ball carrier—the defensive end should charge to the inside on this switch call. Versus a split end, the outside linebackers should aim for the nose of the offensive tackle (refer to diagrams 5-35, 5-36a, 5-36b, 5-36c, 5-36d).

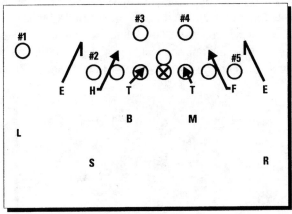

DIAGRAM 5-35

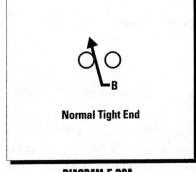

Normal Tight End

DIAGRAM 5-36A

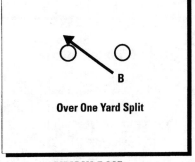

Over One Yard Split

DIAGRAM 5-36B

Less Than One Yard Split

DIAGRAM 5-36C

Split End

DIAGRAM 5-36D

As soon as the outside linebackers diagnose the play or get blocked they should adjust their course. It is important that they go underneath (to the inside) the offensive tackle trying to pass block them so that they do not interfere with the rush lanes of the defensive tackle or the defensive end.

The inside linebackers play laterally against all runs and are responsible for the quarterback against a hook-up option (i.e., the quarterback fakes to one of the backs before attacking the corner). For all passes, the inside linebacker away from formation plays #4 cautious man-for-man, and the inside linebacker on the side of the formation plays #3 or curl depending on the coverage (refer to diagram 5-37).

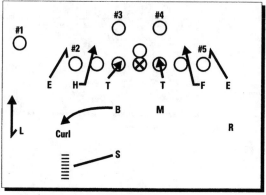

DIAGRAM 5-37

VI. Split 6 Storm Defense

On the snap of the ball, both outside linebackers charge through the inside half of a tight end in a normal alignment. The inside linebacker on the side of formation blitzes, while the inside linebacker away from formation performs barrel maneuver. On a barrel maneuver, the linebacker charges through the inside half of the offensive tackle on the snap. It is important to note that when he hits the penetration point that his shoulders are square to the line of scrimmage (refer to diagram 5-38).

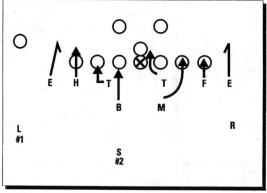

DIAGRAM 5-38

CHAPTER 6

How to Play Linebacker in Special Defenses

Once the basic defense has been learned, it is relatively easy to teach other defenses. Each supplemental defense complements the basic defense, and all play a valuable role within the total defensive package. The purpose of this chapter is to discuss a few of the more commonly used supplemental defenses and to identify the techniques and responsibilities of linebackers who are playing in these defenses.

I. Four-four Rotate Defense
The secondary rotates to the side of the action (refer to diagram 6-1).

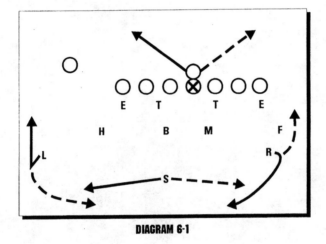

DIAGRAM 6-1

A. Both inside linebackers align and play the same as the Split 6 Rotate Defense.
B. Outside linebackers.
    1. Alignment rules:
       • Align 11/2 yards outside a normally aligned (one yard split) tight end and two yards deep (refer to diagram 6-2).

Once the basic defense has been learned, it is relatively each to teach other defenses.

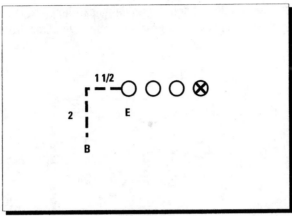

DIAGRAM 6-2

- Line up slightly outside a tight end that is split two yards (refer to diagram 6-3).

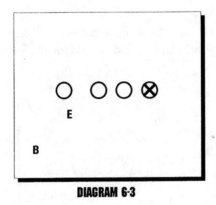

DIAGRAM 6-3

- When an offensive end is split over two yards, all of the adjustments become the same as those for the Split 6 (refer to diagram 6-4)
- Against a tight wing (one that is split not wider than two yards), align same as the Split 6 (refer to diagram 6-4).

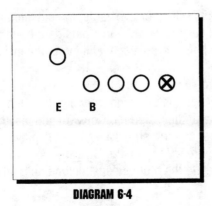

DIAGRAM 6-4

- In the case of a 3-yard split by a wingback, the outside linebacker should line up two yards deep and nose up on the wingback (refer to diagram 6-5).

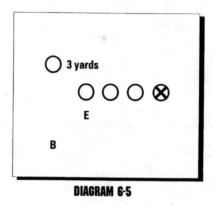

DIAGRAM 6-5

- Against a 5-yard wingback, the outside linebacker should line up two yards deep on the inside half of the wingback (refer to diagram 6-6).

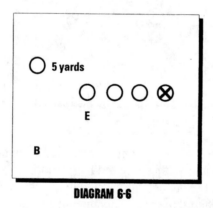

DIAGRAM 6-6

- If a wingback is split over five yards, the outside linebacker should line up in the normal position (1 1/2 yards outside the tight end, two yards deep).
- When off the line of scrimmage, align with the inside foot slightly forward.

2. **Key the ball**
3. **Play versus the run**
    - Provide run support in a straight forward direction two steps if the ball comes. End with the inside foot forward and play high blocks with the inside shoulder and forearm. Make running plays go deep and to the outside and be ready to play that way.
    - If the ball goes to the other side, slide and be ready to play the cutback.

- Against a straight down-the-line option, play the pitch.
- Versus a "hood-up" option, play the quarterback to pitch. Try to string out the quarterback, make him pitch the ball, and then pursue at a proper angle to the ball.

4. **Pass Responsibility**

   Pass responsibility is the same as the Split 6 Rotate Defense except the outside linebacker contains when the ball comes in his direction (refer to diagram 6-7).

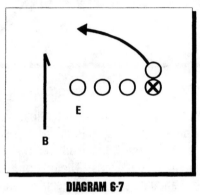

DIAGRAM 6-7

II. **Eagle Rotate Defense**

The secondary rotates to the side of the action (refer to diagram 6-8).

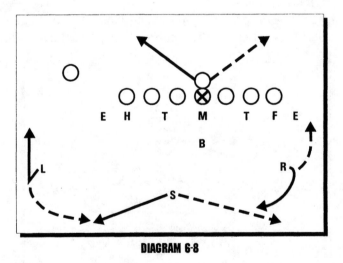

DIAGRAM 6-8

A. The outside linebackers line up and react the same as in the Split 6 Rotate Defense, except they play curl on a straight drop back pass (refer to diagram 6-9).

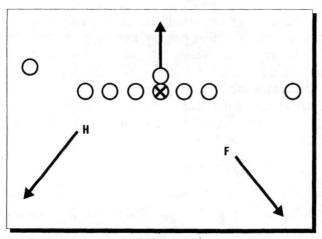

DIAGRAM 6-9

B. The inside linebacker who is stronger but less mobile (referred to as the Mike) lines up on the center in a three or four point stance. He plays square into the center, reads his head, and rushes the passer once the threat of a draw no longer exists. The other inside linebacker (referred to as the Backer) should assume an alignment and adhere to the following basic rules of play:

- Line up three yards deep and stack the offensive center.
- Key the ball and flow to the ball as required in the Split 6 Rotate Defense.
- Against a run action, he should play lateral to the offensive guard and then pursue from inside to outside (refer to diagram 6-10).

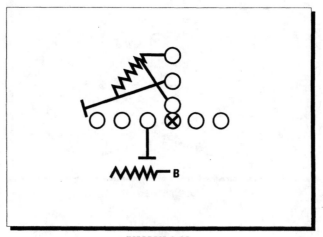

DIAGRAM 6-10

- On an action pass to either side, he should go to the curl zone on the side of the action (refer to diagram 6-11).

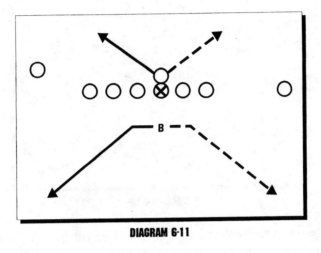

DIAGRAM 6-11

- Against a drop back pass, he should play the middle zone (refer to diagram 6-12).

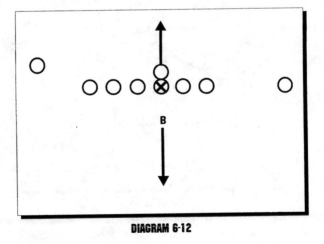

DIAGRAM 6-12

III. Fifty-two Rotate Defense

The secondary rotates only on action to the weak side (refer to diagram 6-13).

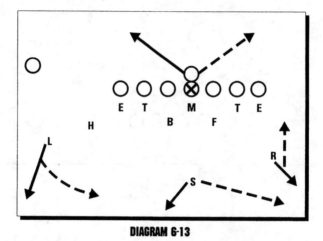

DIAGRAM 6-13

A. The two inside linebackers (Mike and Backer):

- Align nose on the outside eye of the offensive guards at a depth of about 21/2 yards.
- Key in the same manner as the inside linebackers in the Split 6 Rotate Defense.
- Play laterally on run action in either direction. On run action to their side, they play quickly to the outside half of the offensive tackle and then pursue from inside to outside. On run action away from them, they are responsible for any cutbacks (refer to diagram 6-14).

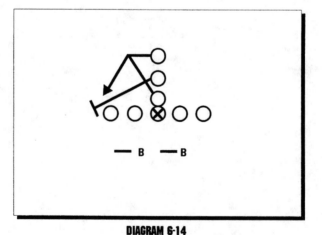

DIAGRAM 6-14

- On action toward their side, Mike and Backer are responsible for plays that come outside the offensive tackle, either the outside veer or the quarterback.

- The Mike and Backer have the same responsibilities against all passes as the inside linebackers in the Split 6 Rotate Defense.
- No adjustment is made when twin receivers are present.

B. The strong outside linebacker (Hero):
1. Align as follows:
- Line up 5 yards outside a normal tight end at a depth of three yards (refer to diagram 6-15).

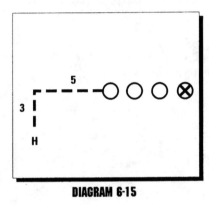

DIAGRAM 6-15

- Against a tight wingback, line up slightly outside the wingback at a depth of two yards (refer to diagram 6-16).

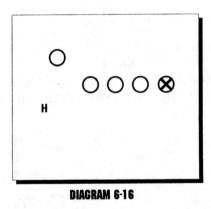

DIAGRAM 6-16

- Align head up on a 3-yard wingback at a depth of three yards (refer to diagram 6-17).

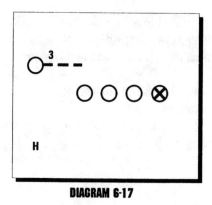

DIAGRAM 6-17

- Line up slightly inside a 5-yard wingback at a depth of three yards (refer to diagram 6-18).

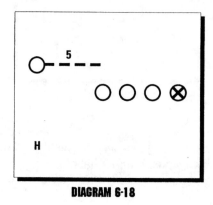

DIAGRAM 6-18

- Align five yards outside the tight end at a depth of three yards against a flanker that is wider than five yards.
- Against two wide receivers to one side, the Hero aligns on the receiver at a depth of three yards (refer to diagram 6-19).

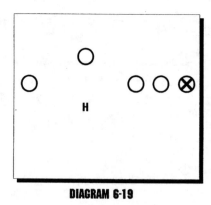

DIAGRAM 6-19

2. **Keys the ball**
3. **Supports straight up versus run action to him**
   He plays with his inside foot forward and plays high blocks with his inside shoulder and forearm. He should make outside plays go deep and to the outside, and be ready to play that way.
4. **Plays the pitch versus all options**
5. **Has the same pass responsibility as in the Split 6 Defense, except he plays the flat zone in the case of an action pass to his side** (refer to diagram 6-20).
6. **No change of responsibility is required versus twin receivers**

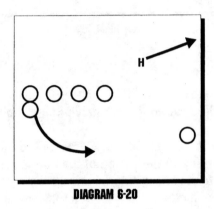

DIAGRAM 6-20

IV. Fifty Rotate Defense

The secondary rotates only on action to the weak side (refer to diagram 6-21).

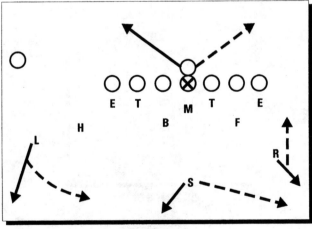

DIAGRAM 6-21

The strong outside linebacker (Hero) aligns and plays the same as in the 52 Rotate Defense. The strong inside linebacker (Backer) plays the same as in the 52 Rotate Defense, except on run action to the weak side when he attacks the guard-center gap (refer to diagram 6-22).

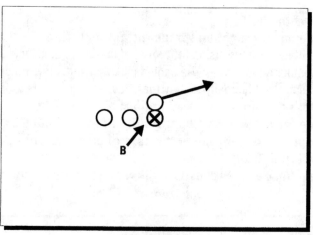

DIAGRAM 6-22

A. **The middle linebacker (Mike):**
   1. **Aligns on the nose of the offensive center and is 11/2 to two yards deep**
   2. **Keys in the same manner as he does in the Split 6 Defense**
   3. **Plays according to the action of the ball versus a run**
      • On action to the strong side, he attacks the guard-center gap and is responsible for the inside veer (refer to diagram 6-23).
   4. **Has the same pass responsibility as he does in the Split 6 Defense.**

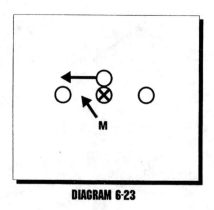

DIAGRAM 6-23

   • On action to the weak side, he slides along the line of scrimmage (refer to diagram 6-24).

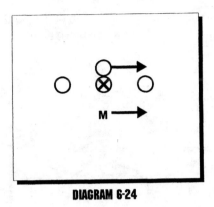

DIAGRAM 6-24

• On action straight at him, he plays square (refer to diagram 6-25).

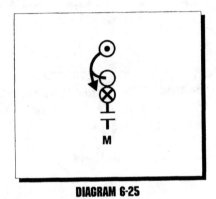

DIAGRAM 6-25

B. The weak side outside linebacker (Fritz):
   1. Aligns nose on the outside eye of the offensive tackle at a depth of 2 1/2 yards.
   2. Keys through the offensive tackle for his first reaction:
      • If the offensive tackle fires straight out, the Fritz plays him square with his inside shoulder (refer to diagram 6-26).

DIAGRAM 6-26

- If the offensive tackle reaches to one side, the Fritz slides and tries to maintain control of the offensive lineman (refer to diagram 6-27).

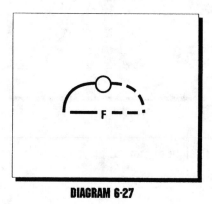

DIAGRAM 6-27

- If the offensive tackle blocks down, the Fritz steps up and is ready to react to the outside if the tight end comes down on him. If the tight end does not come down (refer to diagram 6-28a), he reacts to the inside (refer to diagram 6-28b).

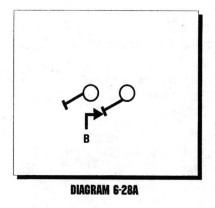

DIAGRAM 6-28A

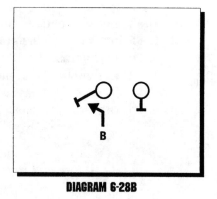

DIAGRAM 6-28B

- If the offensive tackle blocks out, the Fritz steps up and looks to the inside (refer to diagram 6-29).

DIAGRAM 6-29

- If the tackle pulls to one side, the Fritz slides in that direction (refer to diagram6-30).

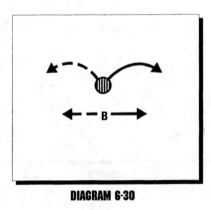

DIAGRAM 6-30

- If the tackle pass blocks, the Fritz reacts to his pass zone (refer to diagram 6-31).

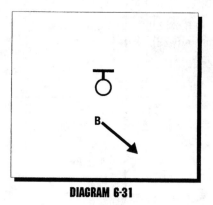

DIAGRAM 6-31

V. Forty Rotate Defense

The secondary rotates only on action to the weak side (refer to diagram 6-32).

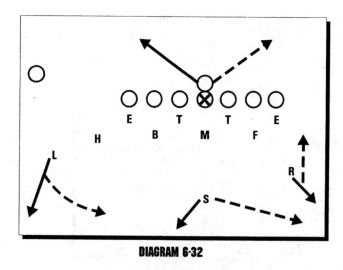

DIAGRAM 6-32

The strong side outside linebacker (Hero) plays the same as he does in 50 and 52 Defenses, while the weak side outside linebacker (Fritz) plays the same as in the 50 Defense. The strong side inside linebacker (Backer) plays the same as the Fritz in the 50 Defense, except he plays the curl zone on an action pass to his side (refer to diagram 6-33).

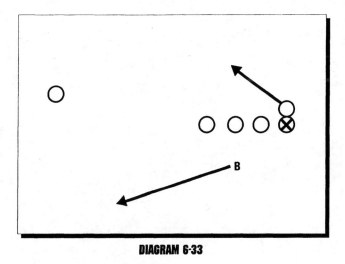

DIAGRAM 6-33

The inside linebacker on the center (Mike) plays the same as in the 50 Defense except he moves laterally on any action to the strong side (refer to diagram 6-34).

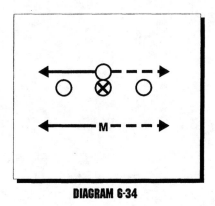

DIAGRAM 6-34

Summary

Several possible defensive adjustments have been presented in this section in order to provide you with a better understanding of the multiplicity of defensive schemes and responsibilities of linebackers in those schemes. It is not necessary to use all of these adjustments in a game or during an entire season. It is your responsibility as the coach to identify which defenses best meet your situational needs and best suit your personnel. Finally, it is critical that you take the appropriate steps to ensure that every linebacker who plays for you knows and carries out his responsibilities on every defensive scheme. The success of your team's defensive efforts are dependent upon the ability of each player to properly execute his duties on every play from scrimmage.

CHAPTER 7

What Are the Fundamentals and Principles of Defensive Play?

Coaches should always attempt to avoid misunderstandings and to be consistent in their expectations regarding their players. One of the best ways to accomplish this goal is to develop a list of fundamentals and principles of defensive play. Many of the most commonly accepted basic fundamentals have been passed down from one successful coach to another. Research, playing experience, common sense, and film analysis have all played integral parts in contributing new ideas. After the proper methods and techniques have been determined, the players should be drilled to develop proficiency in the requisite skills and techniques.

It is very important to realize that many ways exist to develop skill proficiency in your athletes. By the same token, you should keep in mind that a fine line separates a disciplined approach and making robots out of your players. We believe that the best approach for developing linebackers is one in which they are trained to perform, within certain parameters, with a high degree of recklessness. In order to accomplish this goal, it is imperative that certain generic gridiron fundamentals—such as stance, movement and tackling—must be developed before the techniques specific to position play.

Stance and Movement

When in the combat zone (i.e., close proximity to blockers, receivers, and/or ball carriers), it is necessary for a defensive player to be in a good hitting position. The appropriate position for each individual may vary slightly due to differences in body builds but a list of general guidelines concerning what constitutes a proper stance should include the following:

- His feet should be at least shoulder width apart or slightly wider.
- His toes should be pointed straight forward.
- The weight of his body should be on the toes and balls of his feet but his heels should not be off the ground.
- His knees should be bent and positioned slightly beyond his feet.
- His legs should be tense (muscles contracted) and ready for sudden movement.
- The player should bend forward at the waist so that his head and chest are positioned slightly beyond his knees.
- His hands should be positioned slightly outside the knee joint with his palms facing inward and parallel to his leg.
- His neck should be bulled (i.e., tented) with his eyes looking up at the target.
- His upper body should be relaxed in order to facilitate ease of movement but should become tense immediately before contact.

When moving in the combat area, whether it is forward, lateral, or on an angle, the defender should try to stay very close to the recommended hitting position—the arms should move freely. Having a proper stance becomes increasingly more important the closer a defender is to the offensive players. Defensive linemen must be able to take off explosively yet make quick changes of direction as necessary. They must be able to explode outwards (not up) off of both feet, get under blockers, and continue to accelerate forward upon contact. Linebackers must be able to move efficiently (i.e., not waste motion or effort) in all directions and not raise or lower themselves anymore than necessary while moving. All defenders should strive to be smooth, fluid-moving athletes.

Among the recommended drills for developing the proper stance and movement techniques in players are the following:

- On Command Position Drill — The defender practices getting into a good hitting position.
- Stance Walk Drill — The defender walks in a good hitting position (using opposite hand-foot movement).
- Stance Run Drill — The defender runs in all directions in a good hitting position (to get the feel of going as fast as possible yet under control).
- Move-Stop Drill — The defender moves in various directions, then comes to a stop in a good hitting position, ready to play (sprint - stop, lateral - stop, etc.).
- Sprint-Gather Drill — The defender sprints forward at full speed, then gathers himself, coming under control in a good hitting position.
- Spring-Gather-Attack Drill — Same as sprint-gather drill except after the defender has come under control, he veers off at approximately a 45° angle (in good position) as if attacking a ball carrier.
- Quarter-Eagle Drill — From a good position, the defender makes a quick 90° turn. The defender should not hop, but turn as quickly as possible by pivoting his entire body. The drill should end with a full speed burst (i.e., the defender turns right, turns back to the left, turns left, turns back to the right, and then runs full speed right).

Defensive linemen should work on straight ahead starts, then start and make quick changes of direction after one step (simulating down blocks, reach blocks, etc.). Linebackers should slide and work on their footwork while simulating various blocking schemes. Defensive backs should retreat, then accelerate at the various angles that a ball might be thrown.

The type of movement used by a defensive player is determined to a great extent by the requirements of his position. Among the recommended techniques for moving in various directions are the following:

Lateral Movement

The defender should not raise or lower himself from his initial stance. He should maintain his shoulders relatively parallel (or "square") to the line of scrimmage while moving laterally. The direction in which a defender moves laterally is dictated by a key or the ball.

The first basic lateral movement is the slide or the shuffle. This is the easiest movement from which to change direction because a player's feet never cross. Sometimes it is only necessary to slide once. A systematic analysis of lateral movement shows that the defender leans in the direction to which he wants to go, slides his back foot (the one opposite the direction that he wants to go) in the direction of the body lean, and then slides the lead foot in the direction that he is going. It is very important to note that he does not hop or cross his feet. This movement must be a quick move, with his feet remaining as close to the ground as possible. The defender's elbows should be kept close to his body. Any upper-body motion should be minimized. If play dictates, the defender continues to slide in this same manner.

If sliding is not fast enough, then it may become necessary to run laterally. To run in this manner, the defender should keep his shoulders square and allow his arms to swing naturally. Again, the defender leads with his back foot (the one opposite the direction that he wants to go), but this time he crosses over the other foot (e.g., if going to the left, it is right over, left out).

- The defender should turn his shoulders to run only as a last resort.
- The defender should not waste motion or become overextended.
- The defender may be able to enhance his movement quickness by performing the skills required for his position with an all-out effort. Everything should be performed with a maximum effort, whether it is one slide or a forty-yard sprint; any effort less than maximum can and often does become a bad habit.

Forward Movement

When a linebacker is moving forward, he should employ the following techniques:

- The defender's toes should be pointed straight ahead.
- His weight should be on the balls of his feet.
- He should push (spring) off one foot, paw out with the other.
- As his foot comes down, the defender's body should move forward so that his center of gravity is over his foot as it touches.
- His hands and upper body should be relaxed, with his index finger and thumb cupped. Some players may prefer to move their hands in a paddling-type motion. Regardless of how a player moves his hands, his hands and upper body should be relaxed.
- The defender's elbows should remain close to his sides.

- He should employ his opposite hand in an opposite-foot-movement pattern. As his left foot goes forward, his right hand shoots upward to shoulder height and left hand moves backward towards his hip.
- The defender should bend slightly, flexed (bent) at the waist, with his head tilted slightly downward and his eyes directed straight ahead.
- The defender should try to move as smoothly and fluidly as possible (no wasted motion).
- Finally, the defender should concentrate on moving his feet as fast as possible.

Backward Movement

When the linebacker is moving backward, he should employ the following techniques:

- The defender should pump arms (similar to the way he does when he's moving forward), employing the opposite hand with an opposite-foot-movement pattern.
- He should push off the ball of one foot and paw back with the other foot.
- His upper body should be relaxed, his elbows in, and all movements smooth and fluid.
- Finally, the defender should keep his knees flexed (bent) and lean forward in order to be in a position to be able to change directions quickly.

Shedding Blockers

In playing off blockers, it is important to do only what is required to make a play. A defender's primary objective should be to make tackles, not to destroy blockers. It is critical that the defender stay square, explode without unnecessary effort, after contact be able to move before his offensive opponent (i.e., be the first to move after contact)., react to the blocker's pressure, control the blocker, and come off the block at an angle to meet the ball carrier (most of the time laterally). In order to neutralize a blocker charging above the waist, a defender should:

- Stay square with the blocker, not commit to a slide.
- Take a short step, then drive out and underneath the face mask of the blocker. The defender should get underneath (vertical leverage) the blocker. His hands should be driven underneath the shoulder pads of the blocker. Upon contact, he should lower his hip and buttocks so that his feet are underneath him.
- Not wind up or waste motion, but instead create maximum explosion with a minimum amount of wasted effort — think of "stinging" the blocker.
- Not get overextended, but rather maintain a balanced position.
- Strain upward and into the pressure of the blocker while accelerating his feet upon contact in short, choppy steps.
- Work to get his head up (his back should arch).
- Make an all-out effort to get rid of the blocker. Push (press) and throw off the offensive man. Do not stay blocked! Come off the block laterally and quickly.

Among the additional points which should be emphasized regarding shedding blockers are the following:

- The defender should prevent the blocker from getting a position between himself and the ball carrier.
- The defender should never spin away from the blocker.
- The defender should strain into the pressure of the block, give ground, keep his shoulders square, and take a proper pursuit angle, if a blocker has managed to position himself between the defender and the ball carrier.
- The defender should not go around the block through the "back door" (i.e., the "so-called" easy way).

If a blocker comes down from the outside or out from the inside (at an angle), the defender should stay square and deliver a blow with his forearm and shoulder. The defender should not wind up, but instead make sure that he is in a good hitting position. His lower arm should be flexed (bent) slightly and his elbow driven out from his body. A defender's shoulder and forearm should be underneath the blocker. As always, the defender should strain into the pressure of the blocker, accelerate his feet, stay square, and be ready to give a step and instinctively come off the block at the proper angle.

When a blocker attacks below the waist, the defender should:

- Concentrate on the blocker, while watching the ball carrier out of his periphery.
- React to the blocker's head, slide in the direction of his head, and strive to maintain his position.
- Use his hands to stop the offensive man's charge. The defender's hands should be directed in the area of the offensive player's shoulder pads.
- Flex (bend) his knees, push with his hands, and give with his feet to clear the offensive man's charge.
- Keep his shoulders square and make his second move before the offensive man's charge.
- If necessary, give ground to keep his shoulders square. He should not go around behind the blocker if the offensive man has good position. He should keep moving in the direction that the offensive man is trying to go.
- Be prepared. A good defender has the ability to side and coil at the same time in order to be able to strike a blow (butt).

Tackling

An intense desire to excel, proper body position, and proper balance are essential factors in consistently being able to demonstrate proper tackling techniques. It is recommended that when a defender is making a tackle he should:

- Not raise or lower himself from a good hitting position and stay square when approaching the ball carrier.
- Keep his elbows close to his sides and not wind up.

- Bull (contract) his neck, keep his eyes open, and stay square to the ball carrier upon contact.
- Accelerate his feet with short, choppy steps and wrap his arms around the ball carrier upon contact. His hands should make contact in the area of his opponent's buttocks then slide up as the ball carrier is taken back.
- Keep his head up, back arched, and always try to look at the ball carrier.
- Drive through the ball carrier, while trying to take him back five yards and put him on his back.
- Drive his head in front of a ball carrier that is coming at an angle (not straight ahead) and then strain upward and into the ball carrier, always turning his head into the ball carrier to look at him. The defender should accelerate his feet in the same manner as for a straight-ahead tackle.
- Keep his eyes open when assisting on a tackle so that he doesn't knock off the other tackler.
- Spring from his stance and attempt to meet a ball carrier in the air who is diving to score a touchdown or get a first down.
- In most instances, attack ball carriers in the open field — force the ball carrier to make a decision.
- Use the sideline to his advantage when making a tackle by coming under control, taking away the runner's inside cut, and forcing him out of bounds.

Pursuit

It is important that defensive players approach ball carriers at the proper angles. Using good judgment and taking the proper angle of pursuit can help to overcome the comparative speed advantage which is enjoyed by most offensive backs. When pursuing a ball carrier, some important points for the defender to remember are:

- Inside defenders should try to keep everything on their outside shoulder when the action comes to their side. They should pursue in a lateral direction until the ball carrier has turned upfield and then attack from the inside position.

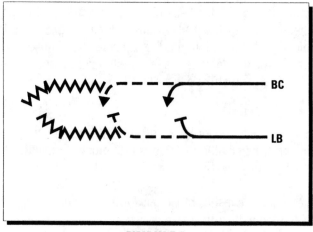

DIAGRAM 7-1

- When a ball carrier goes away from a defender, he should maintain a position slightly to the inside so that he can guard against the cutback.

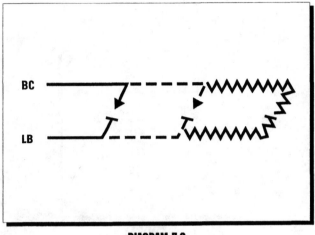

DIAGRAM 7-2

- Attempt to make ball carrier continue to run in a lateral direction. Try not to create a seam so that a back can run upfield.
- Take a steeper angle of pursuit (from the line of scrimmage) in order to save a touchdown when the ball carrier is farther away.

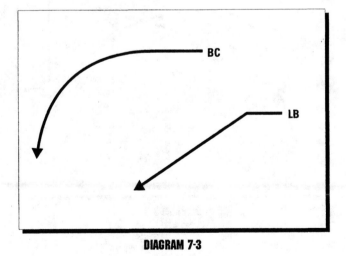

DIAGRAM 7-3

- When playing the quarterback against the option, pursuit should be at least at a flat angle to intersect the ball carrier's path once the quarterback has pitched the ball. If the ball is pitched well out in front of the quarterback, it is necessary to take a steeper angle (from the line of scrimmage) to meet the ball carrier.

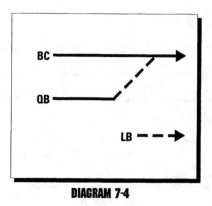

DIAGRAM 7-4

- Outside defenders (playing a flat zone) should attack flare and screen passes from an outside position, attempting to force the ball carrier into the middle of the field.

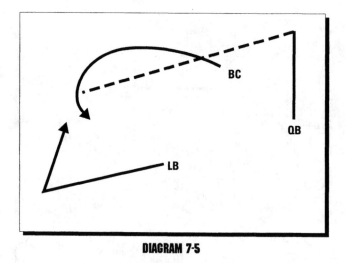

DIAGRAM 7-5

- Defenders should converge on plays to their inside from an outside-in-angle (maintain a fence when aligned on the outside).

Pass Defense (Zone)

Defenders playing zone pass defense position themselves at a relative distance to each other so that they can cover the areas of the field into which a quarterback might want to throw the ball. The linebacker's primary concern is guarding an area of the field between the defensive backfield and the line of scrimmage and reacting to the look of a quarterback. A linebacker playing a zone must also be aware of the positions of potential receivers who might be a threat to his area of responsibility. The recommended techniques for a linebacker playing zone pass defense are:

- As soon as linebacker recognizes a pass play, he should call it out and start moving to his area of responsibility as fast as possible. Assuming a proper depth initially gives him an opportunity to come under better body control when the ball is about to be thrown.
- Most of the time, he should turn and run laterally looking over his shoulder at the quarterback.
- As he is going to his zone area, he should glance for receivers who might be coming into his area, but he should never turn completely away from the ball. He should know where receivers are, yet still be able to react if the quarterback throws quickly into his area or another area.
- He should position himself between the ball and a potential receiver in his zone. Once he has gotten within about three yards of the receiver, he should settle down (stop in a basic hitting position) where he can see both the receiver and the quarterback (match up with the receiver). He should be turned at approximately a 45° angle towards the outside, aligned three yards in front of the receiver and three yards to his inside, concentrating on the ball but watching the receiver out of his periphery, and being ready to react to any throws at an angle that would allow him to intercept the ball. If the receiver breaks to the inside behind the linebacker, he should pivot back to face the ball and react to it.
- If no receiver is in his zone (twelve to fifteen yards deep), he should square his shoulders to the line of scrimmage and begin to back pedal. While running backwards, his weight should be on the balls of his feet, his arms should move as if running, and his elbows should be close to his sides. As he is retreating, he should scan for receivers.
- He should react to all "looks" of the quarterback in his area. When the quarterback looks, he should turn his shoulders and sprint at an angle to make the interception in front of the receiver.
- He should try to catch the ball at its highest point, lock it into his hands, should "fire", and head toward the goal line.
- All of the linebackers should communicate with each other. They should tell the adjacent linebacker if a receiver is crossing into his area.

- If a receiver crosses a linebacker's path, he should be knocked to the ground or at the very least off stride, but the linebacker should not get overextended or ever go out of his way to hit a receiver. The linebacker should not lose his position in attempting to knock down a receiver.
- Once the ball is thrown, all linebackers should be running at full speed toward the ball until it is either intercepted or batted to the ground.

Pass Defense (Man-For-Man)

Defenders playing man-for-man pass coverage should concentrate on the eligible receivers and cover them wherever they might run. Two types of man-to-man pass coverage techniques can be used. The linebacker can play reckless man-for-man coverage when he has help in the deep secondary. Reckless techniques are used to take away the underneath passes (from the line of scrimmage to a depth of about eighteen yards). Cautious man-for-man techniques, on the other hand, are used when the linebacker does not have any help in the deep zones, and must, therefore, protect them. When playing cautious man-for-man pass defense, the linebacker:

- Aligns himself approximately one yard inside the offensive receiver at a depth of about four yards with his inside foot forward.
- Concentrates on the receiver.
- Begins to run backward, leading with his front foot, as the receiver comes forward.
- Tries to maintain a distance of two to three yards between himself and the receiver and maintains a position of one yard to the receiver's inside. As the receiver gets closer to him, he begins to run laterally in order to maintain his position (refer to Insert 7-6).
- Breaks parallel to the receiver's changes of directions, and then gradually gets closer to the receiver as the ball is thrown.
- Must guard against any deep pass.
- Turns his back to the ball in pursuit if the receiver has gotten beyond him, concentrates on the receiver, especially his hands; and turns toward the quarterback to look for the ball when the receiver's hands come up.

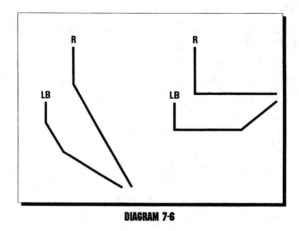

DIAGRAM 7-6

When playing reckless man-for-man with two defensive halfbacks helping in the deep outside zone, the linebacker:

- Aligns in the same manner as when playing cautious man-for-man pass defense.
- Concentrates on the receiver.
- Does not let the receiver go to his inside, jams him if he tries to get inside position.
- If the receiver releases to the outside, waits (does not move) until the receiver reaches his outside shoulder and then turns and jams him with his hands. He also lets the receiver get slightly ahead so that he can cover the underneath passes.
- Chases the receiver, staying to the inside and slightly behind him (refer to Insert 7-7).
- Plays all pass cuts of the receiver from underneath (the side closest to the ball), concentrates on the receiver's hands, and goes for the interception when the receiver reaches for the ball.

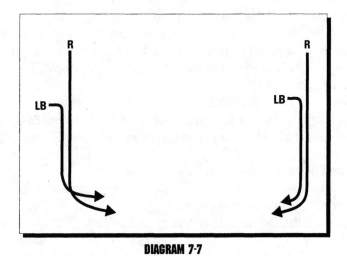

DIAGRAM 7-7

Catching the Ball

Turnovers, specifically interceptions, can have a major impact on the final outcome of a game. For this reason, it is important that linebackers spend ample practice time catching thrown balls. Some of the steps that a player should do when receiving a ball are:

- Concentrate on the ball.
- Look the ball into his hands.
- Do not attempt to run with or look away from the ball until it is firmly in his hands.

- Keep his hands "alert' but not too tense.
- Give with the ball as it contacts his hands.
- Reach out with his hands and move toward the ball when going for an interception.
- Put the ball away (i.e., tuck the point of one end of the ball under his arm covering the other end with his palm and middle fingers).
- Keep his thumbs pointed to the inside if the ball is thrown above his waist.
- Keep his thumbs pointed to the outside if the ball is thrown below his waist.
- Should yell "fire" or some other word to let his teammates know that the ball has been intercepted.

Blitzing

Blitzing can be an effective maneuver to change the normal pattern of linebacker play. When blitzing, the linebacker attacks an offensive area on the snap of the ball. Blitzing is used as an adjustment in an attempt to change the tempo of play, to create a long yardage situation for the offense, or to break the continuity of an offensive drive, to rush the passer — especially if certain blitzes take advantage of an offense's pass-blocking scheme. It is also possible to disrupt blocking assignments or stop certain running plays by blitzing. When blitzing the linebacker should:

- Not alarm the offense by altering his stance or starting too soon.
- Go immediately on the snap of the ball.
- Attempt to penetrate across the line of scrimmage.
- Notice the offensive linemen and the action of the ball and adjust as they are moving (inside linebackers should follow pulling guards, etc.).
- Stay under control.
- React to the pressure of blocks as if he were playing normally.
- Use his hands when rushing the passer (refer to section on Pass Rush).
- Try to get the offensive man turned one way and then go in the opposite direction.
- Not dive (leave his feet) to make a tackle except as a last resort.
- Use his hands when playing lead blockers in the open field where the ball carrier has plenty of running room.
- Try to make the blocker miss or give ground in order to save the touchdown.
- Not become impatient or attempt to make every tackle for a loss of yardage.
- Give ground around piles of blockers and defenders in order to make plays for a two- or three-yard gain instead of creating potential "big plays."

Pass Rush

The ability to rush a passer is predominantly innate, but several general coaching points exist that have been learned over the years through trial and error, including the following:

- Get a great jump on the football. Anticipate, know the situation, study the stances of the opponents.
- Get on a corner if possible.

- Be offensive, attack. Get the offensive player into an awkward body position. Cause him to move either laterally or forward. Get the blocker turned or overextended.
- Outside linebackers should establish a speed rush, while inside players should develop a bull rush.
- Do not get hooked up with the blocker. Strive to keep their hands off of you by slapping, pushing, etc. Use quick fakes, then move upfield.
- Operate with your elbows close to your body; your hands should be positioned inside the hands of your opponent.
- Have a sense of timing. Know when your opponent is off balance, when to push or pull and accelerate by the defender.
- Use the arm-under or over techniques, whichever one is appropriate depending upon your height. Develop a counter move off of your best move (e.g., immediately follow an arm-under move with a "club" maneuver).
- Keep moving upfield, maintain constant pressure on the quarterback.
- Get your hands up when the quarterback is ready to throw the ball. Have a sense of timing, know when to raise your hands. Do not leave your feet until the ball is released.
- Maintain relative position to your teammates who are also rushing. Develop a feel for one another during a dropback pass.
- Recognize the blocking direction and react to the pressure of the block.
- Take care of the immediate problems first.
- Learn to concentrate on blockers while seeing ball carriers out of his periphery.
- Not waste motion and effort.
- Have a sense of timing and know when to exert himself.
- Not be a "robot" or afraid to take a chance in order to make things happen.

CHAPTER 8

Drills — Individual

Through individual drills a linebacker can be instructed in and given the opportunity to practice the fundamentals and principles of proper play. All linebackers should be drilled in these fundamentals so that they are able to develop proper, game-like habits. A well-organized drill can provide the basic foundation for a good performance. All drills should be well-planned by you before going to the practice field. Before practice starts, you should:

- Make a checklist of all of the situations which might occur during a game and make sure that you have designed appropriate drills for improving such areas.
- Understand and clearly define the purpose of every drill.
- Evaluate each drill as to whether it is serving its intended purpose; consult with the players to see what benefits they believe that they are getting out of the drills.
- Devise or emphasize certain drills to address particular problems your players may have or your opponents may present.
- Organize the time allotted for individual skill improvement drills so that the most important objectives are reached.
- Organize the drills according to the number of players involved and the space available.
- Make sure that the necessary equipment for the drills is in the proper place on the field prior to the start of practice.
- Fully explain the drill, its purpose, and the planned rotation before you have your players attempt it.

Once practice begins all the drills should move quickly. The tempo should be quick. Everything should be done with a maximum effort — just as if it were an actual game setting. Structure your drills so that very little standing around occurs. It is usually a good practice to avoid staying on one drill too long. If a player executes the fundamental correctly once, it should be sufficient. You should guard against monotony as much as possible and attempt to instill competition between players whenever possible. You should also indicate the proper techniques to the players; showing them the drill once and have them do it as many times as necessary—if a drill is not done correctly, it should be repeated. It is important, however, not to slow everyone down for the sake of one person. If a player repeatedly performs a drill incorrectly, he should receive individual instruction at a different time.

Movement Drills
All drills should begin with the linebacker(s) in a proper stance. If more than one linebacker is involved, a command of "break" should be used to get them into their

stance. Some of the typical drills that we have used at Penn State to develop a number of highly successful linebackers include the following:

- Lateral Start Drill (one slide) — The purpose of this drill is to teach linebackers the proper techniques for initiating lateral movement.

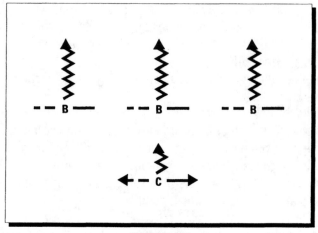

DIAGRAM 8-1

The coach has the linebackers stand in a straight line facing him. With a hand signal, the coach directs them to slide once in the direction that he points and then come to a complete stop, while maintaining their stance. He then repeats a signal for them to move one slide in the same or opposite direction. After a number of slides, the coach points straight ahead and the players turn and run full speed in a straight line for a distance of five yards looking back over their shoulder at the coach.

- Continual Sliding Drill (shuffling) — The purpose of this drill is to teach linebackers the proper techniques for sustaining lateral movement.

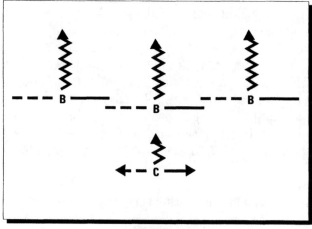

DIAGRAM 8-2

The drill is organized in the same manner as the lateral start drill. The difference between the drills is that when the coach signals to one side, the players continue to slide in that direction until the coach gives them a signal to stop (all while maintaining a good stance). The coach then gives a signal to slide in the opposite direction. After a number of direction changes, the coach signals, and the players sprint in the same manner as the conclusion of the lateral start drill.

- Lateral Run Drill (crossover) — The purpose of this drill is to teach linebackers the proper techniques for running laterally.

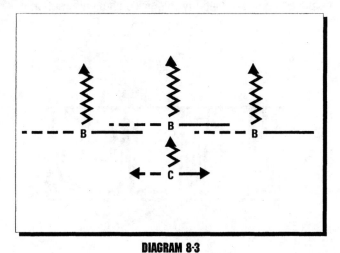

DIAGRAM 8-3

The drill is organized and run in the same manner as the continual sliding drill, except the linebacker runs laterally, keeping his shoulders square, instead of sliding.

- Mirror Crossfield Drill — The purpose of this drill is to train linebackers to mirror a ball carrier by moving laterally at an appropriately relative distance.

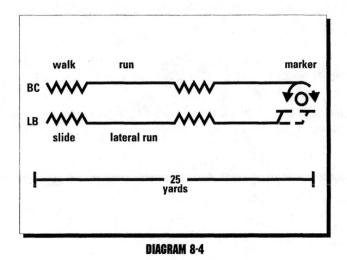

DIAGRAM 8-4

The drill starts with a ball carrier (leader) who walks or sprints in a straight line, changing from one speed to another. He should stay at one speed for at least five yards. When the leader gets to a marker (twenty-five to thirty yards away), he steps forward to either side. The linebacker mirrors the leader by sliding or running laterally, staying slightly behind him, and maintaining the same distance between them (approximately two yards). He stays lateral until the ball carrier turns up, and then tackles him. If done without pads, the drill is ended with a "push-acceleration".

- Change of Direction Race Drills — The purpose of these drills is to evaluate and improve a linebacker's ability to quickly change direction.

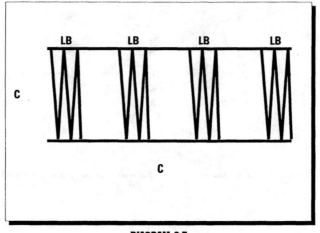

DIAGRAM 8-5

Lateral race - The linebackers stand facing the coach with their near foot on a line. On a hand signal from coach, they run laterally, keeping their shoulders square to the coach until they touch or cross a line five yards five times (a total distance of twenty-five yards). They then repeat the drill facing in the opposite direction.

Forward-backward race - The linebackers stand with both feet behind the line and shoulders parallel to the line. On a signal from the coach, they sprint forward five yards until they touch or cross the next line. Then, they run backwards to the starting line and repeat until they have gone five times (a total of twenty-five yards).

- Around-the-Bag Drill — The purpose of this drill is to develop a linebacker's quickness and teach him to strain into pressure without becoming overextended and to recover by making a second effort.

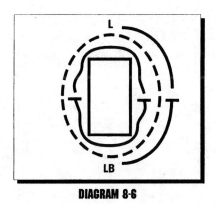

A ball carrier (leader) stands at one end of a long bag that is lying on the ground, while the linebacker stands at the other end and faces the leader. The leader comes forward on one side of the bag and steps into the linebacker. The defender reacts by coming forward on that side of the bag and pushes the leader back a short distance, maintaining his head high with his buttocks lowered to prevent over extension, his back arched, and his feet accelerating with short, choppy steps. Both men recover and race to the other side of the bag and repeat the same procedure. On the last contact (usually the third), the defender strains and pushes the leader back beyond the bag.

- Lateral Fill-Around-The-Bags Drill — The purpose of this drill is the same as that of the "around the bag" drill.

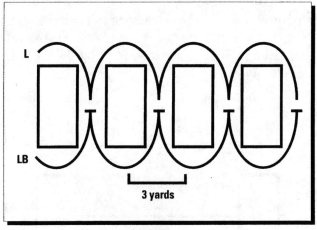

DIAGRAM 8-7

Four or more bags are placed on the ground so that they are parallel to each other. The drill is executed in the same manner as the around-the-bag drill except that after each contact, both the ball carrier (leader) and the defender continue on to the next alley. The defender pushes the leader back after they have gone around the last bag.

- Diamond Mirror Drill — The purpose of this drill is to develop the ability to move backwards and laterally change directions on both the signal of a coach and the action of an opponent.

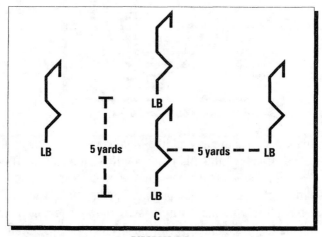

DIAGRAM 8-8

To begin the drill, the linebackers position themselves as diagrammed, facing the coach. The coach first signals the closest defender to run backwards in a straight line, laterally at forty-five degree angles, or forward in a straight line. The other three linebackers do what the first man does, trying to maintain the same distance between each other. On the final signal, everyone sprints full speed to the coach.

- Score Drill (Mirror Dodge) — The purpose of this drill is to develop quickness, sliding ability, and the ability to react to an offensive player without becoming overextended. It also provides an excellent tool to evaluate the movement ability of a defender.

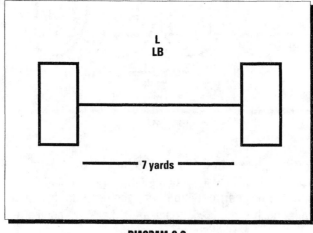

DIAGRAM 8-9

The ball carrier (leader) stands about three to four yards from a line between two long bags lying on the ground. He attempts to cross the line between the two bags as fast as possible by moving laterally and faking the defender who is mirroring him. As soon as he crosses the line, he returns to the starting position and tries to score (by crossing the lines untouched) as many times as possible in a given time limit, usually fifteen to twenty seconds. The defender slides to stay in front of the leader trying to prevent him from scoring. He may use his hands but the emphasis is on moving the feet and not being overextended. To emphasize the importance of moving the feet, the drill is done occasionally with the defender putting his hands behind his back.

Tackling Drills

- Form Tackling Drills (versus a player or a sled) — The purpose of form tackling drills is to teach the proper form in making a tackle.

  Fit - the defender is fitted into the sled (or ball carrier) in the proper contact position. The position that he should end up in upon making contact with the ball carrier.

  Fit and follow through - from the fitted position the defender drives through the sled (or ball carrier) wrapping his arms, keeping his head up, and accelerating his feet.

  The tackle - starting from a good hitting position about three yards away from the sled (or ball carrier), the defender fires into the sled, makes the tackle, and follows through as described.

- Score Tackling Drill — The purpose of this drill is to force the linebacker to move and change directions before making a tackle.

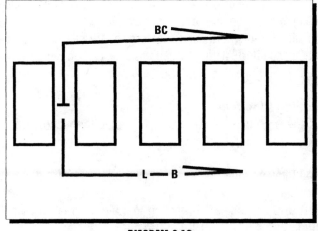

DIAGRAM 8-10

Three to five bags are positioned on the ground parallel to each other about two yards apart. The ball carrier and defender align on opposite sides of the middle bag. The ball carrier runs back and forth between the outside bags and tries to fake the defender. On the command "score", the ball carrier runs straight up the nearest alley. When the command is given, he tries to get across the front edge of the bags. The defender mirrors the ball carrier and attempts to tackle the ball carrier and drive him back before he crosses the front edge of the bags.

- Attack-A-Bag Drill — Similar to the "score tackling drill," the purpose of this drill is to force the linebacker to move and change directions before making a tackle.

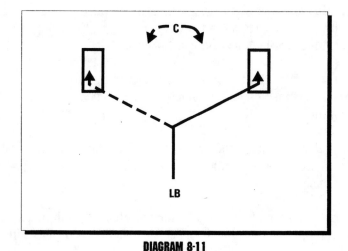

DIAGRAM 8-11

Two bags are positioned about eight yards apart with a coach (player) standing in the middle of the bags. A defender is positioned 10-12 yards away from the bags. The defender moves forward as fast as possible yet in a good position. When he reaches a point approximately five yards from the bags, the coach steps to one side or the other. The defender then angles toward that bag, drives his head across in front, turns into the bag, picks it up, and takes it back five yards. When practicing without pads tackling is simulated with a push-acceleration (the defender places both hands under the leader's shoulders, with his head up, back arched, and feet moving in short, choppy steps).

Drills on Shedding Blockers
The purpose of these drills is to practice and develop the techniques involved in shedding blockers.

- Simulated Blow vs. Air Drill — Hit, accelerate feet, strain, get off the block. (Straight on, angle, etc.)
- Slide-Butt Drill — Slide as if reacting to a blocker then pop as if striking a blow. Slide-Pop, Slide-Pop Drill — Do not cross over.

- Slide-Push-Give Drill — Simulate playing off a low block by sliding, pushing, and giving (all in one synchronized movement). Use a sled, if available.

Combination Drills
- Dive Drill — The purpose of this drill is to have a linebacker learn to play off various types of blocks and make a tackle.

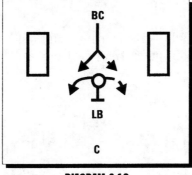

DIAGRAM 8-12

Two bags are laid on the ground parallel to each other approximately five yards apart. An offensive blocker is positioned between the bags with a ball carrier about five yards directly behind him. The linebacker aligns facing the blocker. The coach signals for the blocker either to fire straight ahead or to execute a low block to one side. If the coach points straight ahead, the ball carrier goes to either side of the blocker but stays inside the bag. The offensive blocker then gets involved in the drill. The linebacker plays off the block and makes a tackle.

- Two-man Dive Drill — The purpose of the drill is the same as that of the dive drill, with the exception that more people are involved.

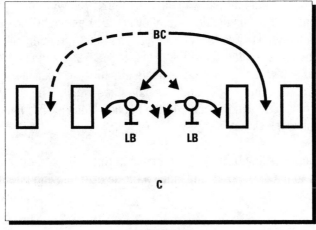

DIAGRAM 8-13

The drill is organized in the same way as the dive drill, except two bags are positioned about three yards outside the other bags, and that there are two blockers and two linebackers involved. The coach signals the type of blocks (same as in dive drill) and the starting count. The coach calls the starting signals. If the blockers go straight ahead, the ball carrier runs forward and must stay within the inside bags. If the blockers position block to one side, the ball carrier goes between the two outside bags in that direction. The linebackers play the blocks and make the tackle whichever way the ball carrier chooses to run.

- Three-On-One Key Drill — The purpose of this drill is to have the linebacker react to a key, play off various types of blocks, and make a tackle.

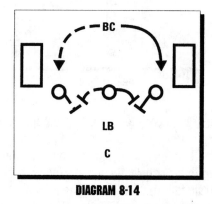

DIAGRAM 8-14

Two bags are laid on the ground parallel to each other and about seven yards apart. Three offensive blockers are positioned alongside each other, between the bags, and in a three- or four-point stance. A ball carrier aligns himself approximately five yards behind the middle blocker and the linebacker starts opposite the middle blocker. The coach signals to one of the blockers and initiates the action with the command "go." If he points to one of the outside blockers, they come at an angle and block the linebacker above the waist. The ball carrier breaks in that direction and stays inside the bags. The linebacker slides, plays the block, and makes the tackle. If the coach points to the middle blocker, he also gives him a direction. On command, the blocker tries to gain position on that side and blocks below the waist. The ball carrier goes to that side and runs between the bag and the outside blocker. The linebacker plays the block and makes the tackle.

- Inside Linebacker Key Drill — The purpose of this drill is to force an inside linebacker to play off blocks and make a tackle after moving laterally.

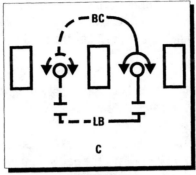

DIAGRAM 8-15

Three bags are laid on the ground parallel to each other, about three yards apart. A blocker is positioned in each of the two alleys in a three- or four-point stance. A ball carrier is positioned about three yards on the opposite side of the middle bag. The coach signals to one side and initiates the action with the command "go." On the command, the ball carrier starts to the signaled side and the blocker comes forward and high blocks the linebacker. The ball carrier breaks anywhere between the two bags. The linebacker slides in the direction of the ball carrier, plays the block, and makes the tackle.

- Deliver-A-Blow Drill — The purpose of this drill is to develop "shock" when delivering a blow, to react to blockers at different angles, and to come off blocks properly.

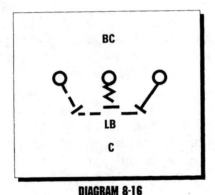

DIAGRAM 8-16

Three offensive blockers are aligned alongside each other with a distance of about one and one-half yards between each man. A ball carrier is positioned about five yards behind the middle blocker, and the linebacker aligns across from the middle blocker and faces him. The coach points to one of the blockers and the designated man blocks the linebacker above the waist. The linebacker reacts to square up on the blocker and delivers a blow. After contact, both players recover to the starting positions as quickly as possible. The coach then points to another blocker and the drill continues. To conclude the drill, the coach raises his hand to one side. On this signal, the ball carrier goes in that direction, while the blocker on that side fires out. The linebacker plays the block and then makes the tackle.

Pass Defense Drills

- Catching Drills — The primary purpose of these drills is to develop and improve a linebacker's ability to catch the football.

  One-hand-catch — The coach and linebacker face each other at varying distances (seven to twelve yards). The ball is thrown to a point above the linebacker's head, where he must catch it with one hand.

  Two-hand-catch — The coach and linebacker face each other at a distance between seven and twenty yards. The ball is thrown to the linebacker so that he must catch it with his hands in various positions.

  Step-forward catch — The ball is thrown to the linebacker in the same manner as the two-hand catch, but the linebacker now comes one or two steps forward to catch the ball at the highest possible point.

  Look — The linebacker stands with his back to the coach at a distance of about ten yards. On the command, "look," the linebacker turns completely around to face the coach, and the ball is thrown. The linebacker steps forward to catch the ball at the highest possible point.

  Concentration — Two players are positioned in front of a linebacker. All of the players face the coach at a distance of approximately ten yards. As the ball is thrown, the two players wave their hands in front of the linebacker but do not touch the ball. The linebacker concentrates and catches the ball.

  Angle interception — Some type of object is placed on the ground at a distance of about seven yards from the linebackers and ten yards from the coach. The linebackers are positioned beyond the object so that they must come forward at various angles to catch the ball. On the signal the linebacker runs towards the marker, the ball is thrown, and the catch is made in front of the marker.

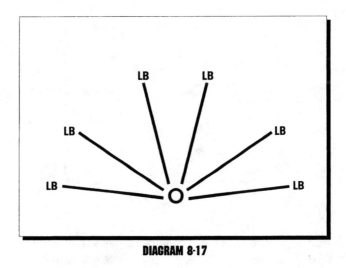

- Semi-Circle Peripheral Vision Drill — The purpose of this drill is to emphasize quick hands, concentration, peripheral vision, and to have fun.

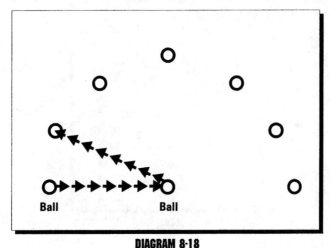

Ball   Ball

The other players form a semi-circle around a designated linebacker. The designated player and the first man in the semi-circle both have footballs. As soon as the designated player passes the ball to the second man, the first player passes the ball to him. This pattern continues around the semi-circle and back to the beginning.

- Match-Up, Zone Drills (A receiver has threatened a linebacker's zone from the outside).ball from a terminal position which the linebacker would have if his zone had been threatened.

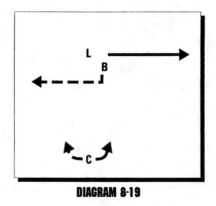

DIAGRAM 8-19

The linebacker looks at the coach and assumes a position with his feet at approximately a 45° angle to the coach. The distance between them is approximately ten yards. On the coach's "look", the linebacker breaks to intercept the ball (pivots back to face the ball or just breaks), shouts "fire," and sprints toward the coach for a distance of five yards.

- Terminal Mirror Drill — The purpose of this drill is to teach the linebacker his proper position in relation to a receiver in his zone and to have him anticipate making an interception.

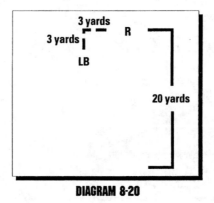

DIAGRAM 8-20

A receiver is positioned twenty yards from the coach and at an angle. The linebacker positions himself between the receiver and the coach so that he can see both of them (as diagrammed). The coach signals to the receiver whether the ball will be thrown on the receiver's break or the coach's look. The linebacker reacts to the first movement of either the coach or the receiver and moves to make the interception. When the ball is caught by the linebacker, he shouts "fire" and springs forward at full speed for five yards.

- Lateral Retreat Mirror Drill — The purpose of this drill is the same as the terminal mirror drill, except that the linebacker must now retreat to his zone.

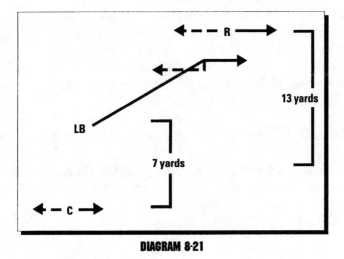

DIAGRAM 8-21

The procedure is the same as for the terminal mirror drill, except that the linebacker aligns himself seven yards from the coach and runs laterally back to the terminal position.

- Lateral Retreat-To-The-Pattern Drill — The purpose of this drill is for the linebacker to develop the ability to retreat to an area, read the offensive pattern and the ball, and make an interception.

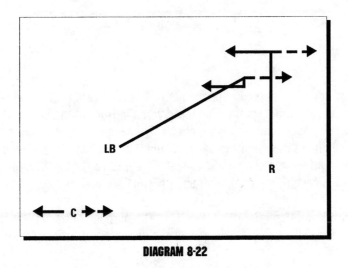

DIAGRAM 8-22

The coach and linebacker line up as they did in the lateral retreat mirror drill and a receiver is positioned about eight to ten yards outside the linebacker. On command, the receiver runs straight down the field about twelve to fifteen yards and breaks in or out. The coach throws the ball on the receiver's break. The linebacker retreats to his terminal position, makes the interception, shouts "fire," and sprints five yards forward at full speed.

- True Zone Drills (a receiver is not threatening the linebacker's zone).

  Terminal back pedal — The purpose of this drill is to learn to back pedal properly and break on the ball at a proper angle to make the interception.

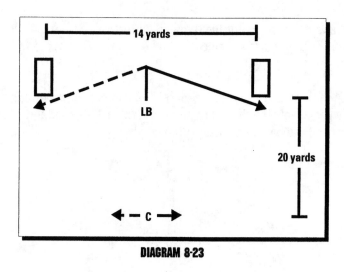

DIAGRAM 8-23

Two bags are positioned upright approximately fourteen yards apart and twenty yards from the coach. A linebacker lines up three yards in front of the bags, midway between the two bags, and facing the coach. On a signal the linebacker back pedals until the coach looks at one of the bags. When the coach looks, the linebacker turns his shoulders and sprints at an angle to make the interception in front of the bag. After the ball is caught, the linebacker shouts "fire" and sprints forward for five yards.

- Lateral Retreat and Back Pedal Drill — The purpose of this drill is the same as the terminal back pedal drill, except the linebacker must now retreat to his zone.

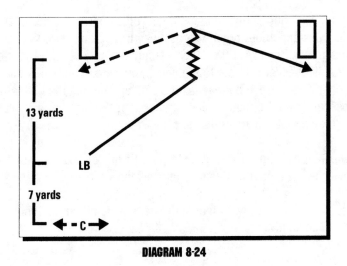

DIAGRAM 8-24

The bags are positioned in the same places as in the terminal back pedal drill. The coach aligns in front of one of the bags at a distance of twenty yards, while the linebacker is seven yards in front of the coach. On a signal the linebacker runs laterally to the terminal spot (twelve yards deep and midway between the bags) and from that point everything is the same as the terminal back pedal.

- Two-Man Tip Drill — The purpose of this drill is to ensure that the linebacker continues to pursue the ball until it hits the ground.

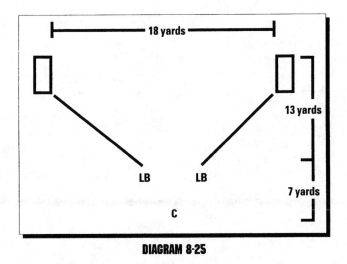

DIAGRAM 8-25

Two bags are positioned upright and eighteen yards apart. The coach stands midway between the bags and about twenty yards away from them. Two linebackers line up alongside each other, and face the coach—approximately seven yards from him. On a signal, each linebacker retreats to the bag on his side. The ball is then thrown to one of the linebackers when he reaches the bag, and he tips the ball into the air. The other linebacker sprints to the ball and catches it at the highest possible point. Both linebackers then sprint full speed to the coach.

- One-On-One Coverage Drill — The purpose of this drill is to cover a receiver man-for-man, both cautiously and aggressively.

The linebacker covers a receiver all over the field using either cautious or aggressive man-for-man techniques.

Fumble Recovery
- Form Recovery Drill — The purpose of this drill is to teach the proper method of falling on a loose football.

A ball is placed three to four yards in front of a linebacker. On command, the linebacker dives forward and reaches out to the ball. On contact, the linebacker pulls the ball to his stomach and curls around the ball, lying on his side to protect himself.

- Competitive Recovery Drill — The purpose of this drill is to teach the linebackers to fight for a loose ball.

Two linebackers line up alongside each other. On command, the linebackers fall forward, touch their chests to the ground, and scramble after a ball that has been thrown between them.

CHAPTER 9

Drills — Group and Team

Football is a team game, requiring individuals to practice in groups or as a team. In order to be successful, players must learn to function as a cohesive unit, working together and anticipating each other's reactions. Group and team drills are designed to create game-like situations that enable individuals to develop proficiency at selected skills and techniques, while fostering group cohesion.

The preparation for all of the group and team drills begins off the field. Coaches should coordinate their efforts. If several coaches are involved in a drill, they should identify the objectives they want to achieve and what role each individual coach must undertake if the drill is to be conducted properly. The coaches should also make sure that they are not duplicating something that has already been covered in another drill or activity.

If a scout team is running plays from cards, every play should be drawn exactly the way it is anticipated the opponents will run the play. The opponent's plays that must be stopped should be run against all the defensive schemes—especially the defenses which are most vulnerable to those plays. The plays should be listed in sequence with the hash mark, formation, and the down and distance of each play recorded. The person responsible for running the plays should have all this information.

During group and team drills, it is also important to emphasize basic fundamentals such as stance and proper techniques. Quickness, hustle, second effort, getting off the ground, and going after loose balls should also be emphasized. The necessary to develop good habits should be emphasized at all times. For instance, even if the ball carriers are not to be taken to the ground, it is still important for the linebacker to accelerate his feet and take the ball carrier back. Everyone should get to the ball by taking the proper lane of pursuit.

During pass drills, a coach should check to see if a receiver could have been knocked to the ground, whether everyone is going to the football, and if the defensive team turns to offense once an interception has been made. Aggressiveness (trying to make a big play) should be emphasized in all drills. Every drill should have a primary purpose (defend outside runs, etc.). "Surprise" plays (a deep pass, etc.) should be run occasionally to keep the defense alert.

Group Pass Defense Drills
In our defensive scheme, five underneath zones are defined. If the ball is in the middle of the field, the flats are seven yards from the sideline and twelve yards deep.

The middle zone is in the middle of the field and is fifteen yards deep. The curls are one yard inside the hash (toward the middle) and are twelve to fifteen yards deep. For every two yards that the ball moves, the zone moves one yard in the same direction. The flat zone, however, is never closer than four yards to the sideline or farther than nine yards from the sideline. The curls are never farther than three yards on either side of the hash mark. The middle zone is never closer than five yards to either hash mark. Linebackers should be reminded that the farther they have to go to their pass zone, the more concerned they should be with width and less concerned with depth. Various drills have been devised to develop the necessary skills to play good pass defense.

- Zone Drill — The purpose of this drill is to define the five underneath pass zones in relation to the ball and the field and have the linebackers retreat to those areas.

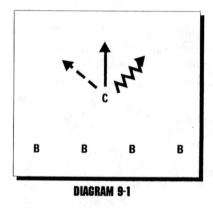

DIAGRAM 9-1

The coach stands in different positions on the field holding a ball. When everyone is ready, he drops straight back, and the linebackers retreat to their proper zones. On the coach's signal they all stop. Each linebacker's position is checked and then the ball is moved to another spot on the field.

- Skeleton Pass Drill — The purpose of this drill is to coordinate the pass defense against the opponent's anticipated pass routes.

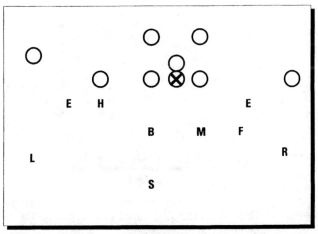

DIAGRAM 9-2

All of the defensive personnel, except the tackles, defend against a quarterback, center, and all eligible receivers. The patterns are run at different positions, in sequence, and against pre-determined defenses.

Defensing the Run

- Half-Line Key Drill — The purpose of this drill is to teach the outside linebackers the proper reaction to the various blocks that they can anticipate.

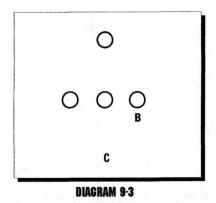

DIAGRAM 9-3

An offensive guard, tackle, tight end, and running back align in their normal positions. An outside linebacker sets up in his normal position with the coach behind him. The coach points out the blocking scheme to the offensive players, and on his command, the offensive players execute the blocking pattern. The linebacker plays off the block and makes the proper reaction.

- Inside Key Drill — The purpose of this drill is to teach the inside linebackers the proper reaction to the various inside plays that they will encounter.

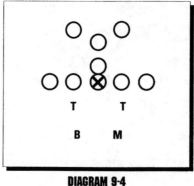

DIAGRAM 9-4

An interior offensive lineman and all of the backs run plays against the defensive tackles and inside linebackers. The plays are run off cards, in sequence, and against pre-determined defenses.

- Outside Play Drill — The purpose of this drill is to teach the proper read, reaction, and pursuit to the various outside plays that are seen.

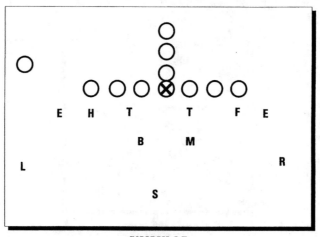

DIAGRAM 9-5

An offensive team runs outside plays against a complete defensive team. The plays are run off cards, in sequence, from different positions on the field, and against pre-determined defenses.

Goal-Line Defense
- Goal-Line Zone Pass Defense Drill — The purpose of this drill is to teach assignments and techniques according to the action of the ball in playing goal-line, zone-pass defense.

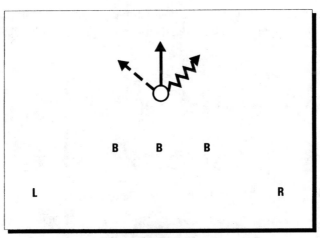

DIAGRAM 9-6

Holding a ball, the coach stands inside the ten-yard line at different positions on the field. When everyone is ready, the coach drops straight back or sprints to either side, while the linebackers retreat to their proper zones. On the coach's signal, they stop. Each linebacker's position is checked; then the ball is moved to another spot on the field.

- Goal-Line Pass Skeleton — The purpose of this drill is to defend against anticipated goal-line passes and to give the linebackers a feel for playing pass defense inside the ten-yard line.

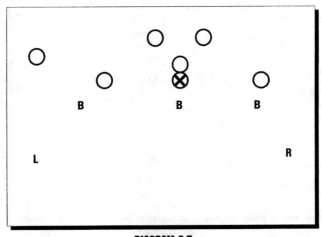

DIAGRAM 9-7

Offensive backs and receivers run patterns against those linebackers involved in goal-line pass coverage. The plays are run from the ten-yard line to the goal-line, in sequence, off cards, and against pre-determined defenses.

• Goal-Line Corner Run Support Drill — The purpose of this drill is to teach the proper run support techniques against outside runs in a goal-line situation.

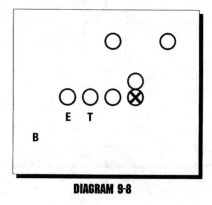

DIAGRAM 9-8

Outside plays are run at a linebacker by an offensive backfield and one-half of an offensive line. The plays are run in sequence and off cards.

• Goal-Line Team Drill — The purpose of this drill is to have the defensive team react as a unit to the anticipated goal-line plays.

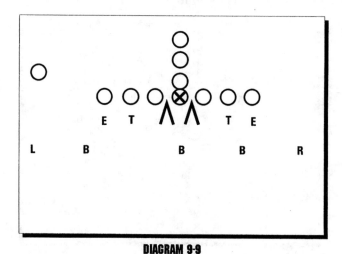

DIAGRAM 9-9

An offensive team runs goal-line plays against the complete defense. The plays are run off cards, in sequence, from different positions on the field, and against pre-determined defenses.

Pursuit
- Skeleton Pursuit Drill — The purpose of this drill is to teach the linebackers the proper angles of pursuit and of convergence on the ball.

The coach or quarterback, two running backs, and two wide receivers run three plays at the linebackers. Each play is first walked through, including the defensive pursuit lanes, then is run at full speed. The first play is a simple down-the-line option where the quarterback comes along the line of scrimmage and pitches the ball to the nearer back. The ball carrier runs for the sideline, then turns toward the goal-line. All linebackers must take the proper lane of pursuit and touch the ball carrier. Next, the quarterback drops back and throws a flare pass to one of the backs. The ball carrier heads for the goal-line, and the linebackers converge and touch him. Finally, the quarterback throws the ball out to one of the wide receivers, and the linebackers pursue and touch the runner.

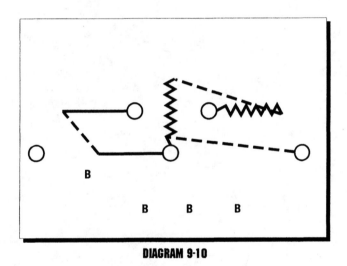

DIAGRAM 9-10

Special Problems
If an opponent's offense presents a special dilemma to the defense, a drill can be organized to emphasize some of their best plays. It might be an option period, an inside running period, a period for screens and delays, or other types of passes, etc.

Teamwork
- Thud Drill — The purpose of this drill is to present game situations to the linebackers and condition them to the tempo of the game.

This practice period involves an entire offensive and defensive team. The plays are run off cards, in sequence, from different positions on the field, and against pre-determined defenses. The down and distance is called out for every play, and the ball is moved down the field. The plays are run quickly, and everyone must hustle in and out of the huddle. The blocking is full speed, but the ball carrier is not taken to the ground. Special situations such as "get the ball back" defense and "two minutes to go" defense are practiced during this period. One sequence usually comprises ten to fourteen plays.

CHAPTER 10

How to Keep Your Players' Minds in the Game

While it is important to practice well, a team must also perform well. Many players respond differently in a game situation; some rise to the occasion, while others seem to become too nervous to function effectively. Still others enjoy the thrill of a crowd and play much better than expected. Most great players have uncanny timing and natural instincts for the "big play." Because it appears that the majority of these characteristics are primarily innate, the coach has little or no control over them.

It is important, however, that coaches and players talk as much as possible about each game situation and the little things that might make the difference between success and failure. First, it is necessary that the players be able to recognize the most common plays that will be run by their opponent and understand the blocking schemes that go with those plays. Next , the players should be able to recognize offensive formations and backfield sets and know the characteristics of each. Finally, the players should be aware of down and distance situations, offensive strategy, big plays, field position, and critical situations.

The Opponent's Basic Plays

As a general rule, each of your opponents will exhibit certain offensive tendencies. Accordingly, each of these teams has specific plays that it tends to run in particular situations. These plays should be identified and defined so that everyone has a thorough understanding of these plays. A few of the offensive plays which are relatively popular (and commonly used) in high school and college football are illustrated in diagrams 10-1 to 10-6.

Most great players have uncanny timing and natural instincts for the "big play."

RUNS

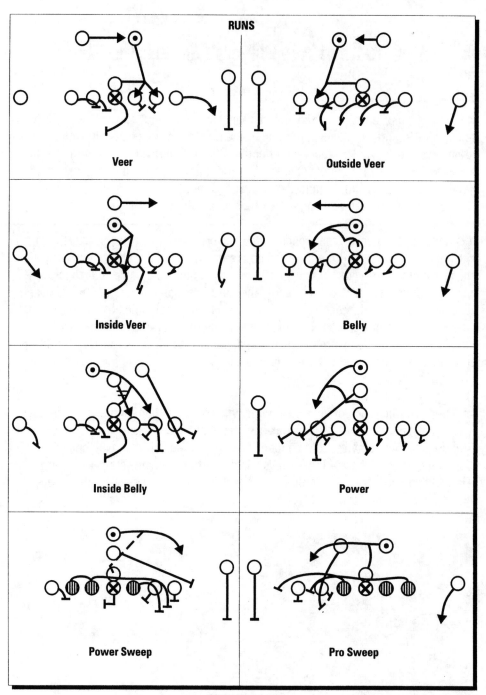

Veer

Outside Veer

Inside Veer

Belly

Inside Belly

Power

Power Sweep

Pro Sweep

DIAGRAM 10-1

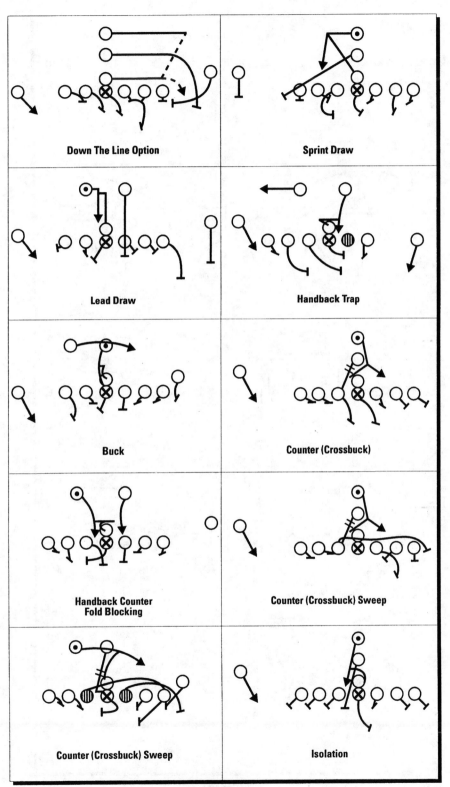

DIAGRAM 10-2

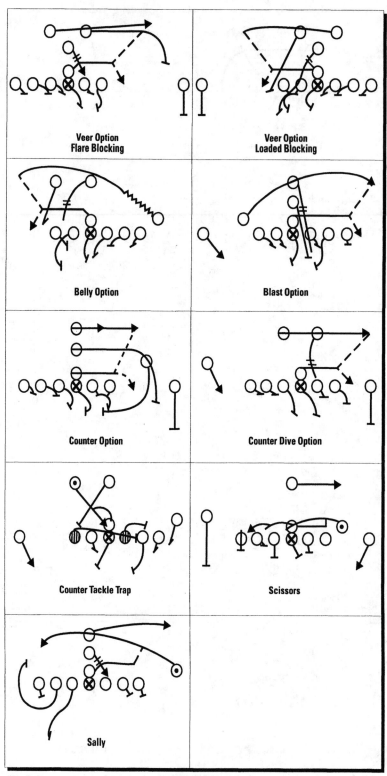

Veer Option
Flare Blocking

Veer Option
Loaded Blocking

Belly Option

Blast Option

Counter Option

Counter Dive Option

Counter Tackle Trap

Scissors

Sally

DIAGRAM 10-3

98

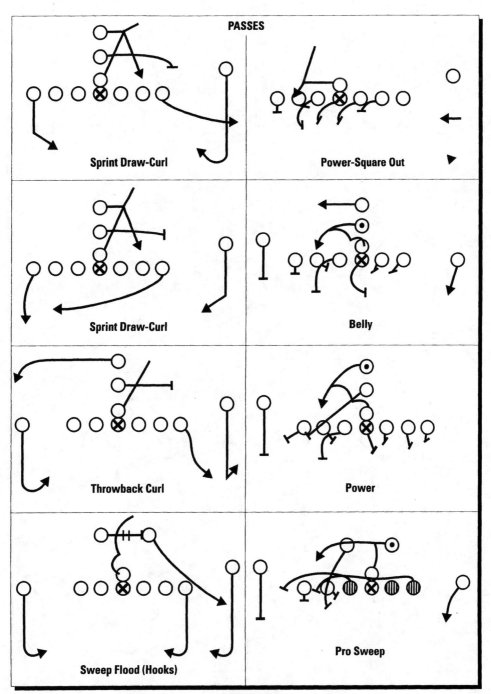

PASSES

Sprint Draw-Curl

Power-Square Out

Sprint Draw-Curl

Belly

Throwback Curl

Power

Sweep Flood (Hooks)

Pro Sweep

DIAGRAM 10-4

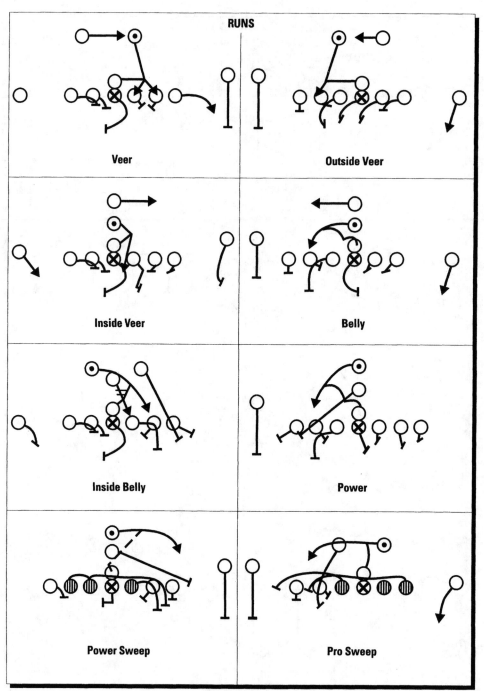

RUNS

Veer

Outside Veer

Inside Veer

Belly

Inside Belly

Power

Power Sweep

Pro Sweep

DIAGRAM 10-5

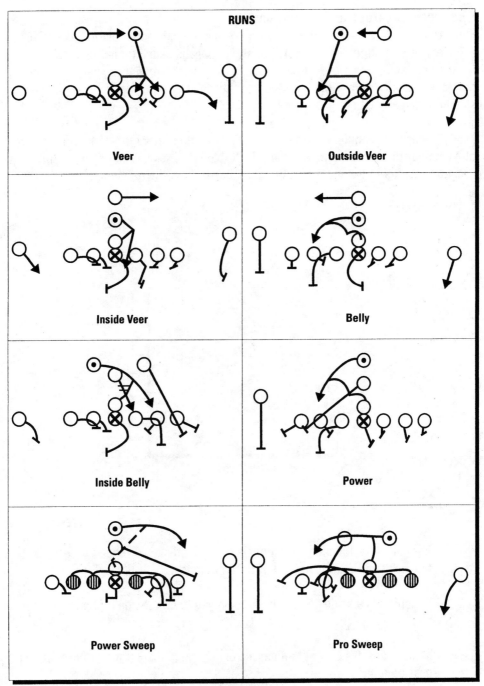

RUNS

Veer

Outside Veer

Inside Veer

Belly

Inside Belly

Power

Power Sweep

Pro Sweep

DIAGRAM 10-6

Understanding Offensive Formations

Linebackers should be alert to a team's offensive tendencies. Most teams will run only certain plays from a particular formation. Because each formation creates a unique problem, a linebacker should be able to adjust more quickly and anticipate better if he can recognize the formation and its basic characteristics. The linebacker should anticipate but not guess.

Inside linebackers should always call out the strength of the formation and the type of backfield set, for example, "Flanker left, 'I' backs". Examples of several of the most common backfield sets and their characteristics include the following:

- "I" backs

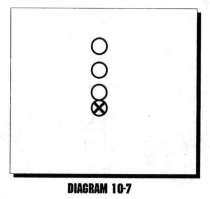

DIAGRAM 10-7

<u>Features:</u>
- Basically, this formation facilitates a tailback-oriented offense. It enables the tailback to hit quickly in a lot of different holes.

- It facilitates a strong outside running game to either side (options, sweeps, etc.).

- Most teams use play action passes or challenge the perimeter with the run-pass option.

- Other basic plays include the sprint draw, isolation, off tackle, buck, veer, veer option, and passes off those plays.

- "T" backs — the halfback is set away from the strength of the formation.

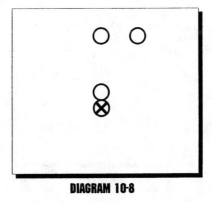

DIAGRAM 10-8

Features:
- The strongest running play is the "belly" to the side of the "set" halfback.

- The set halfback (number two) is more of a pass threat. (Flare control and weak-side flood game).

- Most of the running game to the flanker-side is off counter action.

- "Power" backs — the halfback is set to the strength of the formation.

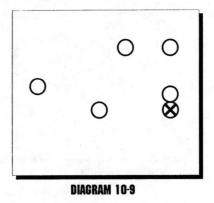

DIAGRAM 10-9

Features:
- The primary purpose of this set is to be able to flood the flanker-side zones (get three receivers out), usually off sprint action or semi-sprint action passes.

- The strongest running plays are the sweep and belly to the flanker- side.

• Full house "T" or solid backfield.

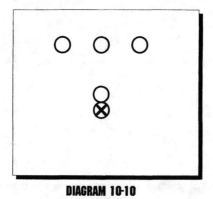

DIAGRAM 10-10

Features:
- This formation facilitates a power running set, usually revolving around the fullback.

- Basic plays off this formation include the belly, the belly option, and the belly pass.

- This formation is very balanced because of the lead back to both sides.

- Counters are easily run because of the closeness of all the backs.

• Power "I".

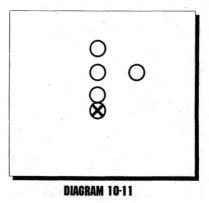

DIAGRAM 10-11

Features:
- This formation offers another power running set.

- This formation is very similar to the "I" with a stronger off tackle game (isolation and belly) to the power side and better counter game away from the strength of the formation.

- The isolation and the blast option are the basic plays away from the strength of the formation.

- "Wishbone."

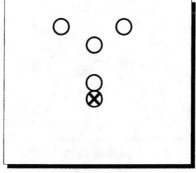

DIAGRAM 10-12

Features:
- This formation is very similar to the fullhouse "T" except that everything is quicker. The backs are in better position to run the option and to get to either side quickly.

- The passing game comes off play action.

- "Tight" split backs.

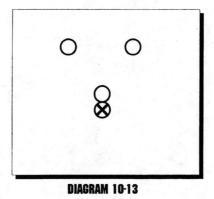

DIAGRAM 10-13

Features:
- This formation is designed to facilitate another quick-hitting offense.

- The basic running plays are the veers, (inside and outside) veer option, counters, counter options, and lead draw.

- The passing game is usually play action (pop pass, boots, etc.)

• "Wide" split backs.

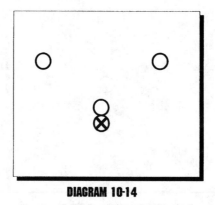

DIAGRAM 10-14

Features:

- This formation primarily offers passing set (five-man out patterns and floods).

- The basic running plays are the pro sweep, quick pitch, trap, and off tackle.

- Play action passes are usually the boot and sweep pass.

Examples of several of the various offensive formations and their characteristics include the following:

• Pro-flanker left.

DIAGRAM 10-15

Features:

- The strongest running plays are usually to the flanker side.

- It is a good passing formation, especially with two wide receivers.

- Wide slot — flanker left.

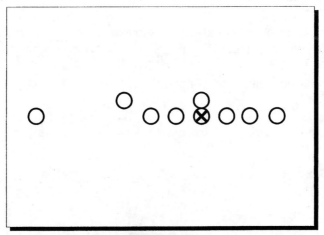

DIAGRAM 10-16

Features:
- The strongest running plays are usually directed away from the flanker side to the tight end.

- The slot creates a good counter game back to the tight end.

- "Twins" — flanker left.

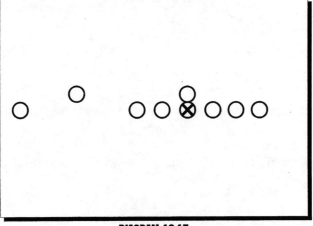

DIAGRAM 10-17

Features:
- This is a commonly used formation which teams employ in an attempt to get their opponents to reduce the eight-man defensive front; it forces you to remove one linebacker.

- The action-pass game to the twins is very strong; many different combinations are possible.

- The most common plays used in this formation are the off tackle and down-the-line option to the twins, and off tackle plays away from the twins.

• "Tight" wing or "tight" slot — flanker left.

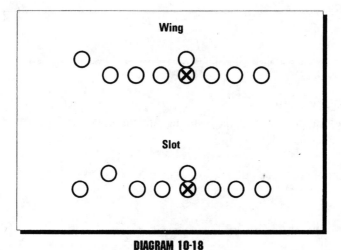

DIAGRAM 10-18

Features:
- This formation facilitates a strong running game (sweeps, etc.) to the wing or slot.

- Most teams like to sprint out and throw back off this formation in the passing

• "Tight" double wing.

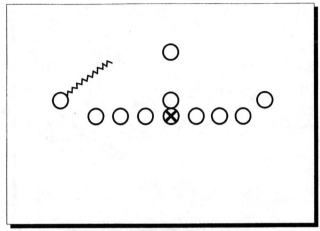

DIAGRAM 10-19

Features:
- This formation is designed to facilitate a misdirection offense with the guards pulling quite often.

- The basic plays are counters (counter sweep, etc.), traps, the belly option, and power sweep.

- The passing game is off action, mostly counter and boot action.

• "Pro" double wing.

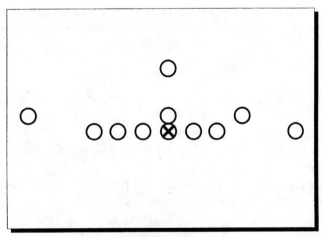

DIAGRAM 10-20

Features:
- This formation basically a passing formation (four quick receivers).

- The most frequently thrown passes off of this formation are floods, delays, and deep passes.

- The running game is limited without motion. Most teams run the draw, trap, and down the line option.

- "Trips."

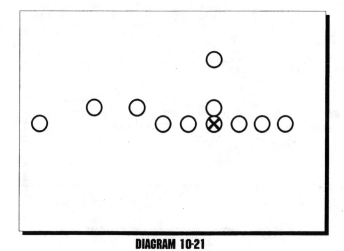

DIAGRAM 10-21

Features:
- This formation is a passing formation, primarily used to flood the formation ("trips") side.

- As a running formation, it is usually limited to a sweep or trap.

Game Situations
Linebackers should be aware of many different situations which arise during a game. They should be alert and flexible, and able to rapidly adjust their play. While each team has its own personality, several general guidelines exist which linebackers should adhere to during a game:

- Anticipate run or pass and adjust your alignment in the obvious situation.
- Anticipate, but do not guess; big defensive plays come about by recognition and going full speed on every play.
- Do not let your opponent out of the defense's four-down area (i.e., keep them inside their thirty-five yard line).
- Come up with a "big play" between the thirty-five yard lines. Try not to let them get into their four-down area with ease.
- Realize that once your opponent crosses your thirty-five yard line, he is in four-down territory.
  Most teams will use their most consistent plays and stay patient; the closer that they get to the goal-line, the tougher it gets to make yardage. Near the goal-line, the defense has less area to defend against the pass and as a result can, play more aggressively against the run.
- Know the score and the amount of time remaining.

Many games are won or lost in the last two minutes. The following factors are important to remember when trying to prevent a score:

- Be aware of what it will take for the opponent to win (a touchdown or a field goal).
- The outside linebackers should go out on the wide receivers if they are playing the flat zone.
  Inside linebackers should deepen.
- The outside linebackers should think of covering square outs and quick outs.
- Everyone should attempt to keep the ball carrier in the field of play.
- Stay alert for a quick line-up. Some opponents will align quickly after a first down. A few might even run two or three plays without huddling.
- Realize that the clock is stopped after a first down until the chains have been moved.
- Don't panic! Equally important, don't give the appearance of losing your composure.

The opposite situation arises when the defense must get the ball back in order to win. In this situation the defensive players should:

- Try to make a "big play." Don't panic, however, and start playing a "helter-skelter" type defense.
- Keep their poise and stay together.
- Get off pile ups quickly and move into/out of the huddle rapidly.
- Know how many time-outs that their team has left and be ready to utilize them wisely. The offense can stop the clock without calling "time-out."
- Realize that the clock stops in certain situations (e.g., when a pass is incomplete, the ball carrier goes out of bounds, or the ball changes hands). A defensive team must not "waste" a "time-out" (i.e., call) in these situations.

CHAPTER 11

How to Prepare for the Moment of Truth — Game Week

For most teams, preparation for a Friday or Saturday game begins the day after the preceding game. All team situations are different however. Various coaching staffs have their own methods of preparations. Certain items, however, should not be overlooked. The basic day-to-day responsibilities of the linebacker coach during the week of the game are outlined as follows:

Sunday
- The scout's report is reviewed to get a general idea about the upcoming opponent.
- All available game films are evaluated.
- A list of the opponent's strengths is developed.
- Charts of the opponent's running plays with the exact blocking schemes are prepared.
- Charts of the underneath pass plays with the exact breaking points of the primary receivers are drawn.
- Notes are made of any special problems, things to emphasize, and adjustments that might be considered.
- The films of Saturday's game are reviewed.
- The linebackers are shown one or two reels of film of their upcoming opponent.
- Several of the pass and running plays frequently used by the upcoming opponent are drawn up for the practice periods on Monday.

Monday
- A discussion of general practice organization involving the linebackers is held.
- The general defensive scheme is reviewed and discussed.
- Any problems with the defenses are analyzed and opened for discussion.
- The practice sessions are organized (i.e., draw up plays, organize drills, etc.)
- A meeting with the linebackers is held prior to practice to present the defenses.
- Practice.
- The assignments for each defense are written up on Monday night (refer to Example 1 at end of this chapter). As the coach writes, he should check for any problems and be contemplating the appropriate adjustments which will be required. The assignments are written to eliminate lengthy meetings and to ensure that the linebackers know their precise assignments.

Tuesday
- The general practice organization involving the linebackers is discussed.
- The defensive game plan is discussed and finalized.

- The writing up of assignments is completed.
- Preparations are made for practice.
- A meeting is held before practice during which the assignment sheets are distributed.
- Practice.
- The coach meets with the linebackers in the evening for a thorough review of the opponent. At this meeting the coach should: Analyze the opponent's offense. Talk about the expected plays and offensive attack. Call out a defense and point out the reaction that the linebacker should make to a certain play when in that defense.
- Point out any tips that might be helpful to the linebackers.

Wednesday
- Organize for practice.
- Discuss all of the problems that have to come to light on the practice field.
- Meet with the linebackers before practice to review or add any adjustments.
- Practice.
- Draw up the opponent's key plays. (Refer to Examples 2a and 2b.)

Thursday
- Organize for practice.
- Tie any remaining loose ends together.
- Make a concerted effort to instill confidence at practice.

Friday
- Special notes (things to remember) are prepared for the linebackers. (Refer to Example 3).
- A list is made of the defenses which will be used in the game to include the strengths of each defense and the reasons for using them. (Refer to Example 4).
- A down and distance chart is prepared for the game. This chart includes all of the defenses and a place to record on which down the defenses are used during the game. (Refer to Example 5).
- Each linebacker should pre-play the game mentally to think of how he will react to some of the problems which might arise during the game.
- A thorough review session is held with the linebackers.

A SAMPLE ASSIGNMENT SHEET FOR AN INSIDE LINEBACKER
(Example 1)

Defense — 6 Rotate.
- Alignment — Boundary or right.
- Key — Near triangle, ball flow.
- Play vs. run —
  - -Move to nose up on offensive tackle versus action. Read the go around, notice the difference between the guard pulling and the isolation.
  - -Attack the nose of the center on action away; meet with your inside shoulder.
  - -Stay square versus fold block.
- Pass responsibility —
  - -Go to curl on action to you.
  - -Play curl versus dropback.
  - -Start center scrape then go to middle on action away from you.
- Option responsibility - Veer.
- Adjustments — Contain versus action to twins; play quarterback versus the option.

Defense — 6 Tough Rotate.
- Align and play same as 6 Rotate except inside versus a dropback pass.

Defense — 6 Blitz.
- Alignment — Same as 6 Rotate.
- Play — Charge straight upfield on the snap (read as you go).

Defense — 67 Rotate.
- Alignment — Stack the defensive tackle on the boundary or right side.
- Play — Same as 6 Rotate except:
  Play inside versus a dropback pass.
  Play quarterback versus the option.
  Against twins, play the middle versus pass.

Defense — State.
- Alignment — Nose on the outside eye of the open field or the left guard.
- Key — Guard, for first movement.
- Play vs. run — Play lateral on action to either side.
- Pass responsibility —
  - -Play the action-side curl versus sprint out to either side.
  - -Play inside versus a dropback pass.
- Adjustments — Versus two wide receivers opposite, the defense goes to 67 Rotate.

Defense — 8 Gun and 8 Blow Rotate.
- Alignment — Same as 6 Rotate.
- Key — Same as 6 rotate.
- Play vs. run — Quickly move to the corner versus action to you; slide on action away.
- Option responsibility — Quarterback.
- Pass responsibility — Same as 67 Rotate.
- Adjustments — Same as 67 Rotate.

A SAMPLE SHEET OF KEY INSIDE RUNS AND BLOCKING SCHEMES
(Example 2a)

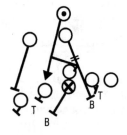 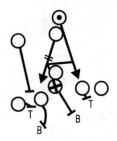 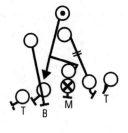

Meet square and tough with inside shoulder.

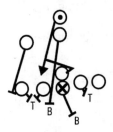 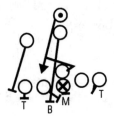

Isolation

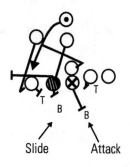

Slide   Attack

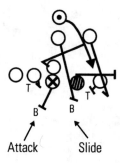

Attack   Slide

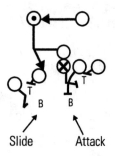

Slide   Attack

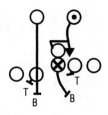 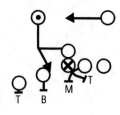

A SAMPLE SHEET OF KEY PASSES
(Example 2b)

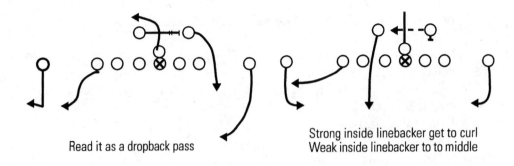

Read it as a dropback pass

Strong inside linebacker get to curl
Weak inside linebacker to to middle

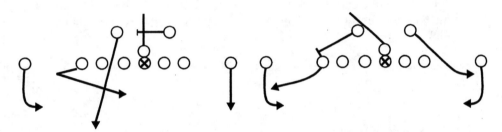

Hang for delay when tight end doesn't go flat

"Mike" must get back to throwback curl

Action-side inside linebacker must get to the curl
Outside linebackers should hang to help
in the wide curl

Same as previous sample

A SAMPLE SHEET OF SPECIAL NOTES
(Example 3)

- Shift only set formation.
- Hero — Remember on 87 Rotate and 6 Tough Rotate to play — curl versus an action pass to a split end.
- Backer — Remember to go to curl versus an action pass — to either side when in the State Defense.
- Fritz — Remember on 6 Tough Rotate and State to play — curl versus an action pass to a split end.
- Twins adjustments:
  Outside linebackers move out except in 6 Go and State Bullets.
  Fritz must always play curl.
  Hero plays flat except when in 6 Blitz, play curl.
  Inside linebackers contain if necessary on all 8's and 6's.
- Double wing adjustments:
  All passes are played as dropback, except on 8 Gun and 8 Blow the outside linebackers must go on action to them. The inside linebackers should go to the curl.

A SAMPLE DEFENSE AND EVALUATION SHEET
(Example 4)

- 8 Rotate.
  A good all around defense that should be sound against everything. Some concern may exist regarding a deep pass when in a "Sam" adjustment.
- 6 Rotate.
  Good versus the outside veer to a tight end. It is a good "change up" versus twins — better versus the pass; not as good versus the down-the-line option.
- 57 Rotate.
  Helps the pass defense if beating rotation. Provides a "change up" versus the "I" running game. Is questionable versus much flanker into the sideline.
- 57 Switch.
  "Change up" versus 5-man-out pass game.
- 52 Rotate.
  Tightens up the inside. Is an excellent pass coverage and is better than 57 versus flanker into the sideline.
- 52 Gap Rotate.
  Helps on running game to the weak side.
- State.
  Tightens the inside running game and is balanced. Is not a very good pass defense.
- 6 Short
  Should be used in desperation to handle the underneath pass zones.
- 52 Gap Tough Rotate.
  Short yardage defense.
- 6 Blitz.
  "Change up" versus inside running and pass game.
- 6 Gun.
  Is our best all-around defense, especially versus boot passing game.
- 6 Storm.
  To be used in desperation.
- Prevent.
  Last play defense.

DOWN AND DISTANCE CHART
(Example 5)

DOWN

Defense	1	2	3	4
8 Rotate				
6 Rotate				
57 Rotate				
57				
52 Rotate				
52 Gap Route				
State				
52 Gap Tough Rotate				
6 Blitz				
6 Gun				
6 Storm				
Prevent				

CHAPTER 12

How to Deal With the Moment of Truth — Game Day

The basic alignment in the Penn State multiple defensive scheme is the Split 6. The numerous variations of the Split 6 Defense and the role that linebackers play in these defenses are outlined as follows:Game day is the players' day. A coach's duties on game day will vary from one staff to another. However, some common responsibilities pertaining to the linebackers exist. Essentially, the linebacker coach should make himself available should any problems arise. He should answer all questions that the players might have. Occasionally, he may remind them of some specific points to remember but will do so without causing any confusion or uncertainty (remember: do not "overcoach"). Every coach approaches each game slightly differently. In general, however, all coaches should make certain that their players are alert without being tense. The basic objective is to make each player feel as though he is well-prepared and ready to make an all-out effort, regardless of who his opponent might be.

One of the responsibilities of the linebacker coach is to "warm up" the linebackers. It is important that the players begin to "sweat" and prepare themselves both physically and mentally for the upcoming contest. In most situations, the various phases of the warm-up period for linebackers involve the following steps:

- Stretch as a team.
- Five or six minutes of pass defense drill:
  - terminal back pedal.
  - lateral start.
  - angle interception.
- Movement drills:
  - lateral start.
  - continual sliding.
  - lateral run.
- Work with a partner:
  - low blocks.
  - bounce the shoulders.
  - form tackles.
- Deliver the blow drill.
- Fumble recovery drill.

Once the game begins, the linebacker coach must try to remember to:
- Remain as focused, yet as objective, as possible.
- Work with and utilize the other assistant coaches.
- Know the defenses and the situations in which they are being used.

- Evaluate the defense, particularly the play of the linebackers.
- Record any mistakes or problems (recognize the opponent's plays that are hurting the team).
- Discuss these mistakes or problems with the linebackers when they come off the field.
- Confer with the other coaches if problems have been identified which need their input.
- Review mistakes and problems during halftime, make the appropriate adjustments, and review what is expected to happen in the second half of the game.

CHAPTER 13

How to Evaluate Your Players' Performance

Following every game, the coach should evaluate the game films. This review is usually done on the Sunday immediately following a Saturday game. The purpose of this undertaking is to evaluate techniques, coaching decisions, and personnel in order to make sure that the right people are being played in the appropriate positions and situations. After reviewing the films, the coach should have identified each player's mistakes, the steps which should be taken to correct these mistakes, and how each player has contributed to the total effort. It is important also that the players have some knowledge of the results of the evaluations of their performance. If a player has performed well, a report of this fact can serve as an incentive and provide motivation; if a player has performed poorly, he should know what mistakes he made so that he (together with his coach) can take steps
correct them.

An elaborate or complex performance grading system is neither necessary nor particularly worthwhile. With so many variables in grading, it is very difficult to be completely objective. Certain intangibles, such as how one player complements another, literally cannot be measured. The grading system can be used to help make personnel decisions but should not be the only factor. An elaborate evaluation system should not be used since it would require a fair amount of time to grade, and thereby possibly detracting from the time available to prepare for the next opponent. In most instances (at the collegiate level particularly), it is also not necessary to have signs, gimmicks, or rewards — evaluation sheets given to the individual player are usually sufficient.

The linebacker evaluation sheet should be designed so that each linebacker has the results of his performance on one sheet of paper (refer to Figure 13-1). Space should be provided for:

- The total number of plays.
- The number of unassisted tackles made (i.e., the linebacker would have made the tackle without assistance).
- The number of assisted tackles made (i.e., The linebacker contributed to the tackle).
- The number of "great hits" (i.e., a superior tackle).
- The number of "bonus plays:"
  - causing a fumble.
  - recovering a loose ball.
  - making a tackle for a three or more yard loss.

- making an interception.
  - deflecting a pass.
  - blocking a kick.
  - making a crucial play (i.e., a key tackle in a short yardage situation, a touchdown saving tackle, etc.).
  - making a tackle inside the opponent's twenty yard line on a kickoff.
  - making a tackle on a punt for no gain.
  - making a tackle for a safety.
- The number of "loafs" (i.e., anytime that the ball is in play and the linebacker is not going full speed).
- The number of poor plays (i.e., violating a principle and not making the play, missing a tackle, not using good judgment, etc.)
- Comments:
  - pertinent remarks about the linebacker's performance.
  - critical statements about incorrect play.
  - suggestions for improvement and correction of mistakes.
  - a good comment about a job well done (i.e., only exceptional performance or effort).
  - a general statement of the overall performance.

CHAPTER 14

How to Condition Your Players: Fit to Win

In order for a linebacker to reach his full athletic potential, he must become as physically fit as his personal genetics will allow. Dedicated participation in a sound conditioning program will ensure that an individual reaches his "physical fitness" potential, and, in turn, help him to reach his true potential as a linebacker. A comprehensive conditioning program for linebackers should include activities aimed at improving:

- Muscular power
- Running speed
- Anaerobic capacity
- Aerobic capacity
- Agility
- Quickness

Muscular Power
Football, particularly the position of linebacker, requires the demonstration of muscular power (frequently referred to as explosive strength or explosiveness). Unfortunately, many coaches do not understand what muscular power really is. Power is the rate at which work is performed, it is not just speed of movement nor is it simply muscular strength. It can be represented by the equation:

$$\text{Power} = (\text{Force X Distance})/\text{Time}$$

From this equation, it is quite evident that power is dependent upon the interaction of three factors: strength (force), speed (time) and flexibility (distance). Muscular power can be enhanced by improving any one of the three factors without adversely affecting the other two.

Factors Contributing to Power

Strength (Force). Strength is simply the ability to exert muscular force. It is primarily determined by the ability of each muscle fiber to generate force and the ability of the nerves to stimulate a large number o muscle fibers. Proper strength training develops individual muscle fibers and enables the body to recruit an increased number of fibers at any given time.

Strength training for power does not mean fast or explosive training. The speed at which an individual executes his strength exercises has little or no beneficial effect on speed of movement or strength development. Additionally, explosive training significantly increases the amount of stress placed on the connective tissues, thereby increasing the individual's injury potential. High intensity (high-tension) training is proper strength training (i.e., training with relatively heavy weightloads in a controlled manner).

In order to develop maximum strength, an athlete should: (1) lift and lower resistances in a controlled manner to ensure that the exercising muscle—not momentum—is responsible for executing the movement; (2) exercise the muscle through its full range of motion to ensure that flexibility is maintained and that the muscle strengthened at all joint angles; (3) include exercises for all the major muscle groups of the body; this will increase overall body strength and will help to prevent injuries by maintaining muscle balance; and (4) progressively increase resistances as muscular adaptation occurs over time.

Speed (Time). The time required for force application is most closely related to speed of movement. Speed of movement is a very complex factor that requires precise coordination between the nervous and muscular systems. It is highly dependent upon the development of efficient motor neuron pathways. Therefore, speed of movement can be enhanced by improving coordination, efficiency of movement, and timing. It requires endless hours of repetitive, skill-specific training to improve one's coordination, efficiency of movement and timing. Skill-specific training is critical for increasing speed and subsequently power.

Movement speed for a particular athletic event depends primarily on inherited neuromuscular factors, and secondarily on quality skill practice. Athletes should practice their skills through the particular activity's range of motion, concentrating on the optimal sequence of events to fine tune their coordination and timing. For best results, skills should be practiced exactly as they will be performed in competition.

Flexibility (Distance). The distance component of the power equation can be limited by an individual's functional range of motion. For example, the velocity at which athletes throw different objects (baseballs, footballs, javelins, etc.) can be severely limited by poor shoulder girdle flexibility. Joint range of motion can be improved through proper strength and flexibility training.

A static stretching (i.e., slowly stretching a muscle past its normal length and holding the stretch) program can be used to improve joint flexibility. The intensity of the exercises for the slow, static stretching should be just below the pain threshold of the individual. A sound program will include exercises for each of the major muscle groups of the body.

In the initial stages of a static stretching program, the stretched position should be held for approximately 10-15 seconds. As flexibility improves, the stretched position can be held for up to a maximum of 60 seconds for each repetition. The total length of time for the workout will be roughly 10 minutes, depending on the number of exercises performed. Proper stretching can significantly improve an individual's joint flexibility. Improved joint flexibility can increase power by enabling an athlete to apply force over a greater distance and usually with more ease and fluidity.

Running Speed

Running speed is primarily a function of stride frequency and stride length. Stride frequency can be defined as the number of steps you take when running for a given length of time or distance. It is a direct reflection of the speed with which you are able to move your limbs. The ability to move the limbs at an increased velocity relies on two factors: fiber type composition of the muscles providing the limb movement, and the neurological efficiency of the involved muscle groups (i.e., the nervous system's ability to transmit impulses from the brain to the receptors in the contracting muscles). Not much can be done to dramatically alter a player's genetic components; however, through proper training, functional capabilities can be enhanced. Stride length is the distance you can cover with each stride. Stride length requires functional strength (i.e., ability to apply force through the range of motion) of the extensor muscles of the hips, knees, and ankles. The individual should also possess sufficient flexibility in the joints involved to allow a greater range of motion and fluidity. An effective program to develop sprinting speed should include work in three distinct areas: strength training, flexibility training, and quality sprint training. Speed is basically a result of the rapid application of force by muscular contractions and is an important component of muscular power.

Strength Training. In order to maintain balance between muscle groups, a properly designed strength training program should include exercises for all the major muscular structures of the body. To develop leg strength for sprinting, all muscle groups of the lower body should be trained, including the gluteals, quadriceps, hamstrings, hip flexors, adductors/abductors, gastrocnemius, and soleus muscles. A limited number of sets should be performed with rep ranges varying according to the desired result. The relationship between muscular strength and muscular endurance can be expressed by using the concept of the repetition continuum. Using rep ranges toward the lower end of the continuum (6-8 reps) emphasizes muscular strength, while the rep ranges greater than 10-12, enhance muscular endurance to a greater degree. To develop muscular strength for sprinting, the number of repetitions should be kept toward the lower end of the continuum, in the range of 6-10. It is important to keep in mind, however, that the lower the rep range used, the heavier the resistance loads, and consequently, the greater potential of injury. Throughout the training year, the repetition ranges utilized may change to increase muscular strength and muscular endurance while also introducing variety into the program. Each repetition should be performed at a controlled speed of movement for all exercises. As the muscles which provide leg drive become stronger, their ability to overcome inertia and accelerate the body mass increases, thus enhancing the athlete's potential for speed.

Flexibility Training. A proper strength training program will increase the muscles' ability to exert force. As stated before, however, this functional strength must be exerted through an appropriate range of motion. Flexibility training should include static stretching of the muscle groups of the lower body, as well as running drills to increase dynamic flexibility and facilitate a relaxed running style. Static stretching should be performed both before (following a warm-up) and especially after the running workout. There are a number of form running drills that may be included in the program. Drills we have utilized at Penn State include high knees, heel kicks, power skips, and arm action drills.

Quality Sprinting. The ability to sprint is an athletic event in itself and requires precise coordination of agonists/antagonists via specific motor pathways. The principle of specificity states that in order to "fine tune" the motor pathways required to perform a given skill, an individual should practice the skill exactly as it will be performed in competition. In other words, by increasing the coordination of the muscle groups involved in sprinting, speed of movement of these body segments will increase. An athlete can spend time performing various running drills to increase dynamic flexibility and to enhance proper technique, but to provide an effective training stimulus, the program must ultimately include maximal speed sprints. Generally, the length of the sprints is determined by the requirements of the particular event. For the sport of football, distances ranging from 10 yards up to 50-60 yards are appropriate. Initially, a limited number of repetitions (generally between 4 and 10) should be performed. As conditioning levels improve, a greater number of sprints may be completed. The key ingredient is the quality of work. All quality sprints should be run full speed (95-100% effort) with complete recovery allowed between repetitions. If the recovery time between sprints is not sufficient, sprint times will increase and hence the intensity of training declines. When the heart returns to 130 beats per minute, the athlete is probably approaching nearing adequate recovery. This is not an absolute reality. Individuals will respond differently, depending upon their level of training. The bottom line is that an athlete should feel almost fully recovered before sprinting again.

Anaerobic Capacity
Anaerobic conditioning (sometimes referred to as "sprint conditioning") is necessary to increase an individual's ability to perform repeated maximal bursts of activity interspersed with periods of rest. The goal of the anaerobic conditioning portion of the workout is to overload the anaerobic system to increase the ability of the body to supply energy (ATP) to the muscles in the absence of oxygen. During anaerobic conditioning, the intensity of effort will be high, but because of the increased amount of exercise and shorter rest intervals, the absolute speed of the repetitions may not be as high as in "speed" sprinting. The goal is to place an effective metabolic demand on the athlete rather than worrying about maximal speed repeats. In order to train the anaerobic system, exercise intervals should be kept below two minutes because aerobic energy stores are increasingly called upon as exercise intervals increase in duration. If the exercise intervals used are 30 seconds or longer, the rest intervals

on the athlete rather than worrying about maximal speed repeats. In order to train the anaerobic system, exercise intervals should be kept below two minutes because aerobic energy stores are increasingly called upon as exercise intervals increase in duration. If the exercise intervals used are 30 seconds or longer, the rest intervals should be initially set at three to four times as long. As conditioning improves, this exercise/rest ratio may decrease to 1-to-1 or even 1-to- 1/2, in order to provide progressive overload. If the sprint distances chosen are 20 seconds or less, recovery periods should be limited to 10-15 seconds. The sprint distances chosen will depend on the demands of the sport or position. Keep in mind that it is difficult to "condition" the athlete with very short sprints. Sprints shorter than 20 yards should be used for agilities and other position-specific drills. For sprint conditioning purposes, distances at least 20 yards or greater are most effective. The total number of repetitions performed in the sprint conditioning period will depend on the length of the exercise interval (sprint distance). Increasing the amount of exercise is another method to provide progressive overload. Remember that the total volume (amount) of exercise will be greater than that performed during the quality sprint portion of the workout. As the number of repetitions increases, they can be segmented in order to allow an extended rest period (2-10 minutes) between sets.

Aerobic Capacity
Aerobic capacity refers to the ability of an individual to use oxygen during prolonged and strenuous exercise. An athlete's ability to recover from all-out, intermittent bursts of activity is highly related to his aerobic capacity. All factors considered, a football player with a high aerobic capacity will be able to perform longer, with less fatigue, and at a higher level of functioning than one with a low aerobic capacity.

A football player can significantly improve his aerobic capacity by adhering to the following basic guidelines:

- Engage in continuous, dynamic activities that involve the large muscles of the body (e.g., running, cycling, stair climbing, etc.)
- Exercise at a level of intensity that is equivalent to 70-85% of maximum capacity (i.e., a training of between 150-175 beats per minute for most high school-age and college-age football players).
- Sustain the aerobic activity for a duration of at least 20 minutes but not more than 60 minutes.
- Perform the aerobic activity three to five times per week.

Agility
Agility, like speed, is largely influenced by the precise coordination that occurs between the muscular and nervous systems. In order for an athlete to experience optimal improvement in agility, the agility drills performed during training should mimic skills the athlete must perform in competition (drills involving agility can been found in Chapters 8 and 9). The remark of the old football coach upon watching

players perform the traditional tire drill during practice illustrates a proper view of agility drills: "We don't have tires on the football fields for games in our conference."

Quickness

Response time is the time required for an individual to initiate a response to a specific stimulus and to move part of his body from one point to another. Coaches often refer to this motor skill as "quickness". Obviously, this is a highly valuable trait for football players. Like agility, the most effective methods for improving an athlete's quickness are general conditioning and specificity training. To enhance quickness, an athlete should adhere to the following general principles:

- Place a demand on all involved systems.
- Regular practice of all specific skills
- Engage in a sound strength training program.

CHAPTER 15

Eat to Compete: Nutrition For Football

Research has shown that coaches can be important sources of nutrition information for athletes—particularly the adolescent athlete. Because the nutritional habits that an individual develops in high school usually continue throughout his college athletic career and into adulthood, it is critical that coaches encourage their athletes to adhere to sound nutritional practices. While almost all available data on the subject indicates that no single food will make an individual into a champion, a corresponding amount of evidence suggest that poor nutritional habits can—in fact—prevent an athlete from playing up to his genetic potential. Besides the effect on an individual's gridiron performance, an unsound diet will also have a negative affect on a player's health—an impact of profound importance.

In order to be able to offer sound advice concerning nutrition fundamentals, a coach should be able to address and answer the following three questions (issues) with his players:

- What should be included in a training diet?
- What should be eaten the day before a game?
- What should be eaten for a pre-game meal?

The Training Diet

Calories for growth, development, basal metabolism, and physical activity are derived from three main sources: carbohydrates, protein and fat. While it is true that alcohol can contribute many calories to an individual's diet, this drug is not a useful source of calories for competitive athletes (or for anyone else for that matter).

Since the major energy source for muscular contraction is derived from stored carbohydrates in the form of liver and muscle glycogen, the diet should be high in carbohydrates. A diet that is 55 to 60% carbohydrates will maintain glycogen stores during the training season. When too little carbohydrate is eaten, these stores become low. After several days on a low carbohydrate diet in combination with daily two-hour workouts, muscle glycogen levels can decrease to less than 50% of normal. These low levels can contribute to feelings of tiredness, soreness, and general fatigue. If humans had to depend only on their glycogen stores to support daily living activities, we would run out of energy in less than 24 hours. Because of this inadequate amount and because athletes rely on these stores for the majority of their energy expenditure, a diet high in carbohydrate is necessary.

Not only is it recommended that an athlete's diet be high in carbohydrates, but the sources of his carbohydrates should be mostly complex carbohydrate or starch. Foods such as pasta, bread, muffins, bagels, rice, potatoes, and cereals are recommended rather than foods high in simple sugar. While it is true that sweet foods such as soda pop, candy, and desserts contribute to glycogen stores, these foods do not contain other essential vitamins and minerals. For this reason, athletes are encouraged to eat the more nutrient dense, starch foods rather than sweets to build muscle glycogen.

Because any players feel that they need a snack before afternoon practice, they often reach for a candy bar and can of soda. While this sugar snack does provide a feeling of well-being and give "energy" during the early stages of practice, they may find that after about 30 to 60 minutes a feeling of sluggishness sets in . The reason for this sluggishness is that the sugar in the snack does not maintain the blood sugar level as long as a snack would which combines protein, fat, and carbohydrate. A better snack before practice would be a peanut butter and jelly sandwich, cheese and crackers, or a piece of fruit.

Most athletes find it surprising that their protein needs are not as high as they believe. It is true that athletes require more protein than non-athletes. It is also true that growing athletes require more protein than adult athletes. However, the extra food that is eaten to support growth and the athletic activity fulfills the protein needs of the athlete. In this way the athlete is eating both calories and protein for growth and muscle development. An example of how an athlete can fulfill his need for protein is as follows:

T. D. Smith is a 17 year old football player and weighs 190 lbs. (86.4 kilograms). He requires between 1.0 and 1.5 grams of protein per kilogram of body weight. From these calculations then, he needs to eat between 86 and 129 grams of protein each day. T. D. could obtain 110 grams of protein from eating two low-fat yogurts, three ounces of baked chicken breast, one cup of green peas, and four, eight-ounce cartons of skim milk. The vegetable protein contributed by complex carbohydrates will easily push T. D. beyond his actual requirement.

It is not unusual to find that football players consume two to three times the amount of protein that they need to continue to grow and develop more muscle. The research is not clear about the hazards of eating excessive amounts of protein over a long period of time. It is known, however, that excessive consumption of protein is not beneficial for athletes. Two basic arguments exist for encouraging athletes not to consume excessive amounts of protein. First of all, protein that the body does not need is not stored as protein. Depending on the energy needs of the body, this extra protein is stored as fat or used for energy. To use dietary protein as a source of energy is a very inefficient metabolic process. Dietary carbohydrate is a much better source of energy. Secondly, when extra dietary protein is metabolized, its nitrogen protein is excreted in the urine in the form of urea. In order to excrete these large diets increase the athlete's risk of dehydration. For these two reason, it is recommended that approximately 15% of the calories come from the protein in foods.

Many advertisements promote the use of "protein drinks" or "protein powders" for weight gain or increases in muscle mass. These products typically contain both a carbohydrate and a protein source and simply add extra calories to the athlete's diet. It is true that muscular development does not occur without enough calories, but the typical high school or collegiate football player eats enough protein and calories for muscle growth. If a player buys one of these expensive products in the hopes of gaining weight, his money would be better spent by eating "normal food" more often during the day so that he has more opportunities to consume more calories. When liquid supplements are preferred for between meal snacks, instant breakfast drinks made with 2% milk can be used. These instant drinks can be purchased at a supermarket and are much less expensive than weight gain powders.

While weight gain and muscle building powders continue to be advertised, a newer addition to the marketplace is single amino acid supplements. It is true that amino acids are the "building blocks" of proteins since all proteins are made up of amino acids. It is also true that eight are considered to be "essential"—that is, these eight amino acids cannot be made or synthesized by the body and must be eaten. What is not true, however, is that supplements of amino acids are needed by healthy football players. For example, one egg, two eight-ounce cartons of milk and a three-ounce hamburger provides an excess of essential amino acids for a 170 pound young athlete. Unfortunately, however, eating an excessive amount of amino acids can have a negative impact on an athlete. Just as described above, they will not be stored as amino acids in the body, but will be inefficiently utilized or stored as fat. Amino acid supplementation also has the potential to increase the risk of dehydration. Furthermore, they are very expensive.

In the past several years, arginine and ornithine—two amino acids that the body makes plenty of—have been promoted for their growth hormone releasing capabilities. They are advertised to athletes under the guise that in high amounts, these amino acids can stimulate the release of growth hormone from the pituitary gland. It is further believed that extra growth hormone causes larger muscles. The facts about arginine and ornithine are as follows:

- When administered to people with a suspected growth hormone deficiency, these amino acids are used to see if the growth hormone secretion is normal.

- Because the liver quickly metabolizes the extra amino acids not required by the body, it is unlikely that these oral supplements have any effect on growth hormone release.

- Adults with diseases that cause an abnormally large secretion of growth hormone are not necessarily thin or good athletes. Quite to the contrary, they suffer from acromegaly. This disorder causes disfiguring enlargements of the bones of the face, hands and feet. They also sometimes suffer from symptoms similar to those of diabetes.

Similar to the aforementioned discussion on protein, the money spent for these amino acids would be much better spent on high carbohydrate foods to increase muscle glycogen stores.

The final nutrient in the training diet that provides calories is fat. As might be expected, the recommendation for fat consumption for the high school or collegiate football player is lower than what is typically consumed. Many athletes obtain 40% of their calories from fat, although a diet which has a fat content of 30% or lower is recommended. Often calories from fat are not readily obvious. Since one teaspoon of margarine, butter, oil, or mayonnaise contains 45 calories and is pure fat, it is relatively easy to eat much more fat than you would expect. Since foods that are high in complex carbohydrates or starches are not high in fat, an athlete's fat intake normally tends to decrease as he eats more carbohydrates.

Fluids are also an important factor in the training diet. The best fluid replacer for a football player is cool water. Fluids that contain sugar are not emptied from the stomach or intestinal tract as quickly as water. If players believe that they need a sugared beverage, diluting a commercial drink with three parts of water to one part beverage is a good compromise.

Excessive water loss through perspiration can lead to a dangerous situation for a football player. A loss of only 3% of the body weight can lead to impaired performance, while heat exhaustion can begin when 5% of the body's weight has been lost. To avoid this, athletes should be required to drink water before practice, during practice, and after practice. Each one pound of weight lost during practice or a game should be replaced with two cups of water.

The Meals Eaten the Day Before the Game
If a player is eating a diet that is normally high in carbohydrates, he may not need to make any dietary changes the day before a game. Many players use the day before to eat foods high in carbohydrate to maximize their glycogen stores. Since glycogen synthesis takes several hours, there is time to do this the day before, but not the day of a game. Several hours are also needed to ensure maximal hydration of the body. The night before an early afternoon game is also a good time to drink extra water.

The Pre-Game Meal
The purpose of the pre-game meal is two-fold. First of all, it should keep the players from getting hungry during the game. Secondly, the pre-game meal is important to

from getting hungry during the game. Secondly, the pre-game meal is important to provide fluids to maintain or improve the players' hydration status. Beyond these two guidelines, it is difficult to make specific recommendations because many psychological factors have been linked to the pre-game meal. For many players this meal is smaller than other meals. As a standard rule of thumb, most nutritionist recommend that a pre-game meal should contain approximately 500 calories. Furthermore, this meal usually should not contain spicy foods, unless these are typically consumed. It should be low in fat, because fat slows the emptying of the stomach. Food left in the stomach and intestinal tract at the beginning of the game may cause nausea or cramping. Since anxiety and excitement also slow digestion, a high fat meal can add to these gastrointestinal problems. Players who are particularly bothered by anxiety may prefer to drink liquid meals. These are emptied from the stomach faster than a meal of solid food.

Once again, the fluid of choice at the pre-game meal is water. If the team eats together at a restaurant, coaches should request that pitches of cold water be put on the tables. The availability of water may encourage players to refill their glass more often. While coffee, tea, and cola beverages are high in water, these are not recommended because of the caffeine content. Caffeine acts as a diuretic and a central nervous system stimulant. Caffeine can cause water loss from the body and can increase an athlete's level of nervous excitement before the game.

Conclusion
Nutrition recommendations for athletes have undergone dramatic changes in the past fifteen years. Unfortunately, while the amount of interest and research in sports nutrition has greatly increased the knowledge available to coaches and athletes, the level of nutrition misinformation has also flourished. Hopefully, the recommendations, explanations, and ideas presented in this chapter will help you answer your players' questions and contribute to their winning performance.

THE AUTHORS

Jerry Sandusky

Jerry Sandusky is the assistant head coach, defensive coordinator, and inside linebackers coach at Penn State University. Credited with developing several of the most outstanding linebackers in the history of the NFL—Jack Hamm, Shane Conlon, Matt Millen, Greg Buttle, among others, Sandusky is the architect of one of the most renowned and successful college defenses in the country. The success his disciples have experienced in the NFL has earned Penn State the title of "Linebacker U". Since joining Joe Paterno's Nittany Lion's staff in 1969, Penn State has appeared in 24 bowl games. Sandusky is widely regarded as one of the most respected and knowledgeable football coaches in America.

Cedric X. Bryant

Cedric X. Bryant, Ph.D., FACSM serves as the director of sports medicine at StairMaster Sports/Medical Products, L.P. in Kirkland, Washington. Prior to assuming his present position, Dr. Bryant served on the Exercise Science faculties of the United States Military Academy at West Point, Penn State University, and Arizona State University. He is a fellow of ACSM and associate editor of the *ACSM Guidelines for Exercise Testing and Prescription* (Fifth edition). He is the author of numerous books and articles on health and fitness.